WOF
AN ABBEY T

ABBEY THEATRE
OUR FEW AND EVIL DAYS
MARK O'ROWE

Premiered by the Abbey Theatre
on the Abbey stage on 3 October 2014.

The Abbey Theatre gratefully acknowledges
the financial support of the Arts Council of
Ireland and the support of the Department
of the Arts, Heritage and the Gaeltacht.

Writer and Director	Mark O'Rowe
Set Design	Paul Wills
Lighting Design	Paul Keogan
Costume Design	Catherine Fay
Music	Philip Stewart
featuring	Seán Mac Erlaine
Voice Director	Andrea Ainsworth
Casting Director	Kelly Phelan
Assistant Director	Maisie Lee
Stage Manager	Diarmuid O'Quigley
Deputy Stage Manager	Bronagh Doherty
	Anne Kyle
Assistant Stage Manager	Stephen Dempsey
Hair and Make-Up	Val Sherlock
Set Construction	53 Degrees Design Ltd.
Scenic Finishing	Sandra Butler and 53 Degrees Design Ltd
Photography	Sarah Doyle
Graphic Design	Zero-G
Sign Language Interpreter	Amanda Coogan
Audio Description	Louisa Sanfey
	Maureen Portsmouth
Captioning	Ruth McCreery

Audio described and captioned performances are provided by Arts and Disability Ireland with funding from the Arts Council /An Chomhairle Ealaíon.

PLEASE NOTE
That the text of the play which appears in this volume may be changed during the rehearsal process and appear in a slightly altered form in the performance.

ABBEY THEATRE
OUR FEW AND EVIL DAYS
MARK O'ROWE

CAST (IN ALPHABETICAL ORDER)

Gary	Ian-Lloyd Anderson
Margaret	Sinéad Cusack
Michael	Ciarán Hinds
Adele	Charlie Murphy
Dennis	Tom Vaughan-Lawlor

There will be one interval of 20 minutes.

SPECIAL THANKS TO

M·A·C Cosmetics for providing make-up products for Abbey Theatre stage shows

Thank you to Robert Donnelly, Joanna Lozowska, Simon Beresford,
Pádraig Cusask Darragh Garvey and Harvey Norman

ABBEY
THEATRE
AMHARCLANN
NA MAINISTREACH

THE ABBEY THEATRE is Ireland's national theatre. It was founded by W. B. Yeats and Lady Augusta Gregory. Since it first opened its doors in 1904 the theatre has played a vital and often controversial role in the literary, social and cultural life of Ireland.

We place the writer and theatre-maker at the heart of all that we do, commissioning and producing exciting new work and creating discourse and debate on the political, cultural and social issues of the day. Our aim is to present great theatre in a national context so that the stories told on stage have a resonance with artists and audiences alike.

In 1905 the Abbey Theatre first toured internationally and continues to be an ambassador for Irish arts and culture worldwide.

Over the years, the Abbey Theatre has nurtured and premiered the work of major playwrights such as J. M. Synge and Sean O'Casey as well as contemporary classics from Sebastian Barry, Marina Carr, Bernard Farrell, Brian Friel, Thomas Kilroy, Frank McGuinness, Tom MacIntyre, Tom Murphy, Owen McCafferty, Mark O'Rowe and Billy Roche.

We support a new generation of Irish writers at the Abbey Theatre including Richard Dormer, Gary Duggan, Stacey Gregg, Nancy Harris, Shaun Dunne, Elaine Murphy and Carmel Winters.

None of this can happen without our audiences and our supporters. Annie Horniman provided crucial financial support to the Abbey Theatre in its first years. Many others have followed her lead by investing in and supporting our work.

We also gratefully acknowledge the financial support of the Arts Council of Ireland.

IS Í AMHARCLANN NA MAINISTREACH amharclann náisiúnta na hÉireann. W. B. Yeats agus an Bantiarna Augusta Gregory a bhunaigh í. Riamh anall ón uair a osclaíodh a doirse i 1904, ghlac an amharclann ról an-tábhachtach agus, go minic, ról a bhí sách conspóideach, i saol liteartha, sóisialta agus cultúrtha na hÉireann.

Tá an scríobhneoir agus an t-amharclannóir i gcroílár a dhéanaimid anseo san amharclann, trí shaothar nua spreagúil a choimisiúnú agus a léiriú agus trí dhioscúrsa agus díospóireacht a chruthú i dtaobh cheisteanna polaitiúla, cultúrtha agus sóisialta na linne. Is í an aidhm atá againn amharclannaíochta den scoth a láithriú i gcomhthéacs náisiúnta ionas go mbeidh dáimh ag lucht ealaíne agus lucht féachana araon leis na scéalta a bhíonn á n-aithris ar an stáitse.

I 1905 is ea a chuaigh complacht Amharclann na Mainistreach ar camchuairt idirnáisiúnta den chéad uair agus leanann sí i gcónaí de bheith ina hambasadóir ar fud an domhain d'ealaíona agus cultúr na hÉireann.

In imeacht na mblianta, rinne Amharclann na Mainistreach saothar mórdhrámadóirí ar nós J. M. Synge agus Sean O'Casey a chothú agus a chéadléiriú, mar a rinne sí freisin i gcás clasaicí comhaimseartha ó dhrámadóirí amhail Sebastian Barry, Marina Carr, Bernard Farrell, Brian Friel, Thomas Kilroy, Frank McGuinness, Tom MacIntyre, Tom Murphy, Owen McCafferty, Mark O'Rowe agus Billy Roche.

Tugaimid tacaíocht chomh maith don ghlúin nua Scríbhneoirí Éireannacha in Amharclann na Mainistreach, lena n-áirítear Richard Dormer, Gary Duggan, Stacey Gregg, Nancy Harris, Shaun Dunne, Elaine Murphy agus Carmel Winters.

Ní féidir aon ní den chineál sin a thabhairt i gcrích gan ár lucht féachana agus ár lucht tacaíochta. Sholáthair Annie Horniman tacaíocht airgid ríthábhachtach don Mhainistir siar i mblianta tosaigh na hamharclainne. Lean iliomad daoine eile an dea-shampla ceannródaíochta sin uaithi ó shin trí infheistíocht a dhéanamh inár gcuid oibre agus tacaíocht a thabhairt dúinn.

Táimid fíor bhúich don tacaíocht airgeadais atá le fail ón Chomhairle Ealaíon.

Biographies

MARK O'ROWE
WRITER AND DIRECTOR

MARK'S PREVIOUS WORK at the Abbey Theatre includes *Terminus* (2007) and *Made in China* (2001). Other plays include *Crestfall* (Gate Theatre, 2003), *Howie the Rookie* (Bush Theatre, 1999) and *From Both Hips* (Fishamble, 1997). Screenplays include *Broken* (2012), based on the novel by Daniel Clay, *Perrier's Bounty* (2009), *Boy A* (2007), based on the novel by Jonathan Trigell and *Intermission* (2004).

IAN-LLOYD ANDERSON
GARY

IAN'S PREVIOUS WORK at the Abbey Theatre includes *Sive, The Risen People, Major Barbara, Shibari, Alice in Funderland, Macbeth, The Rivals* and *The Resistable Rise of Arturo Ui*. Other theatre work includes *Every Doris Has His Day, Big Ole Piece of Cake* and *Bruising of Clouds* (Fishamble: The New Play Company), *Richard III* (Fast and Loose Theatre Company), *Ride On* and *Observe the Sons of Ulster Marching Towards the Somme* (Livin' Dred Theatre Company), *End Time* (Project Arts Centre), *Danti Dan* (Galloglass Theatre Company), *The Colleen Bawn* (Bedrock Productions and Project Arts Centre), *Bad Sunday* (TILT Theatre Company), *Ferry Tales* and *50 Ways to leave Dun Laoghaire* (BDNC and Carpet Theatre Company). Film and television credits include *The Clinic, Raw* and *Love/Hate* (RTÉ), *The Wild Colonial Boy* (TG4), *Dorothy Mills* (Mars Distribution), *Shadow Dancer* (BBC Films and Element Pictures), *Standby* (Black Sheep Productions) and *Scratch* (Warrior Films).

SINÉAD CUSACK
MARGARET

SINÉAD'S PREVIOUS WORK at the Abbey Theatre includes *Juno and the Paycock* (a co-production between the Abbey Theatre and the National Theatre of Great Britain), *One for the Grave, The Irishwoman of the Year, Yerma, The Conspiracy, Emer Agus an Laoch, Galileo* and *Cathleen Ní Houlihan*. Her theatre work includes *Other Desert Cities* (The Old Vic), *The Birds* (Gate Theatre, Dublin), *The Three Sisters* (Gate Theatre, Dublin / Royal Court), *The Bridge Project, The Cherry Orchard, A Winter's Tale* (Brooklyn Academy of Music / The Old Vic), *Rock and Roll* (Royal Court /West End / Broadway, Olivier Awards – Best Actress Nomination, Tony Awards – Best Actress Nomination), *The Mercy Seat* (Almeida), *Lie of the Mind* (Donmar Warehouse), *Our Lady of Sligo* (Irish Repertory / Broadway, Royal National, Critics' Circle Awards – Best Actress, Evening Standard Awards – Best Actress, NY Drama Desk Award – Best Actress nomination), *The Tower* (Almeida), *The Faith Healer* (Royal Court), *Map of the Heart* (Globe Theatre), *Aristocrats* (Hampstead Theatre),

Anthony and Cleopatra, Macbeth and *Much Ado About Nothing* (RSC and Broadway, Tony Awards – Best Actress Nomination), *The Taming of the Shrew, Peer Gynt, The Custom of the Country, The Merchant of Venice, Richard III, The Maid's Tragedy, As You Like It, Measure for Measure, Children of the Sun* and *Wild Oats* (RSC), *Cyrano de Bergerac* (RSC / Broadway), *Arms and the Man* (Oxford Festival) and *Othello* (Ludlow Festival). Television credits include *Camelot, 37 Days, The Deep, A Room With A View, Home Again, The Strange Case of Sir Arthur Conan Doyle, North and South, Tales From Hollywood, Twelfth Night, Loves Labours Lost, Shadow of a Gunman, The Playboy of the Western World,* and *Trilby* (BBC), *Summer Solstice* (Gate TV), *Poirot: Dead Man's Folly, Midsomer Murders* and *Dad* (ITV), *Have Your Cake and Eat It* (Initial for BBC, RTS Awards – Best Actress), *Mirad A Boy From Bosnia* (Double Exposure), *Oliver's Travels* (Worldwide TV & Film), *God on the Rocks* (Channel 4), *The Henhouse* (BBC Belfast), *Scoop* (LWT), and *Romance: The Black Knight* (Thames). Film credits include *Eliza Graves* (Icon Productions), *Queen and Country* (Merlin Films), *The Sea* (IFTA Best Supporting Actress

Award), *Wrath of the Titans, Cracks* (Appian Films), *Eastern Promises* (Eastern Promises Films Ltd.), *Tiger's Tail* (Lionside Ltd., IFTA – Best Supporting Actress nomination), *V for Vendetta* (Warner Bros.), *Mathilde* (ES Fiction), *I Capture the Castle* (Trademark Films), *The Nephew* (World 2000), *My Mother Frank* (Intrepid Films), *Stealing Beauty* (Lakeshore), *The Sparrow* (Gratafica), *The Cement Garden* (Lorentic Films), *Bad Behaviour* (Parallax Pictures), *Waterland* (Palace Productions), *David Copperfield, Cyrano De Bergerac* (20th Century Fox), *Venus Peter* (BFI), *The Last Remake of Beau Geste* (Universal Studios), *Revenge* (PG Prods for Rank), *Hoffman* (ABPC) and *Alfred the Great* (MGM).

CIARÁN HINDS
MICHAEL

CIARÁN'S PREVIOUS WORK at the Abbey Theatre includes *Juno and the Paycock* (a co-production between the Abbey Theatre and the National Theatre of Great Britain), *The Death of Cuchulainn, The Only Jealousy of Emer, On Baile's Strand, The Green Helmet, At the Hawk's Well, Dialann Ocrais* and *The Death of Humpty Dumpty*. Most recently he has appeared in *The

Night Alive (Conor McPherson at the Donmar, London and Atlantic Theater, New York) and *Cat on a Hot Tin Roof* (Broadway). For the National Theatre he has appeared in *Burnt by the Sun*, *The Seafarer* (Broadway), *Closer* (National Theatre and Broadway) and *Machinale*. Other theatre work includes *The Yalta Game* and *The Birds* (Gate Theatre), *Tis Pity She's a Whore*, *The Importance of Being Earnest* (Druid Theatre), *Field Day* (Lyric Belfast), *Richard III*, *Troilus and Cressida*, *Edward II* and *Two Shakespearean Actors* (RSC), *Simpatico* (Royal Court), *Assassins* (Donmar Theatre), *Mahabharata* (World tour), *Observe the Sons of Ulster Marching Towards the Somme* (Hampstead) and he spent seven seasons at the Citizens' Theatre, Glasgow. Television work includes *Above Suspicion*, *Rome*, *The Mayor of Casterbridge*, *Tales from the Crypt*, *Jane Eyre*, *Ivanhoe*, *The Affair*, *Cold Lazarus*, *Persuasion*, *Sherlock Holmes*, *Prime Suspect 3*, *The Man Who Cried*, *Hostages* and *Investigation: The Birmingham Six*. Films include *Last Days in the Desert*, *Frozen*, *The Sea*, *The Disappearance of Eleanor Rigby*, *Tinker, Tailor, Soldier, Spy*, *The Woman in Black*, *John Carter of Mars*, *The Rite*, *Harry Potter and the Deathly Hallows*, *The Debt*, *Life During Wartime*, *The Eclipse*, *Race to Witch Mountain*, *The Tale of Despereaux*, *Miss Pettigrew Lives for a Day*, *In Bruges*, *There Will Be Blood*, *Margot at the Wedding*, *Nativity*, *A Tiger's Tale*, *Hallam Foe*, *Amazing Grace*, *Munich*, *Miami Vice*, *Mickybo and Me*, *The Phantom of the Opera*, *Lara Croft: The Cradle of Life*, *Calendar Girls*, *Veronica Guerin*, *Road to Perdition*, *Sum of All Fears*, *Weight of Water*, *Titanic Town*, *Oscar and Lucinda*, *Some Mother's Son*, *Circle of Friends*, *December Bride*, *Excalibur* and *The Cook, The Thief, His Wife and Her Lover*. Ciarán trained at the Royal Academy of Dramatic Art.

CHARLIE MURPHY
ADELE

CHARLIE'S PREVIOUS WORK the Abbey Theatre includes *Pygmalion* (Winner of the Irish Times Theatre Award for Best Actress 2011). Other theatre work includes *The Silver Tassie* (Lincoln Center), *Disco Pigs* (The Young Vic), *Big Maggie* (Druid and tour), *4.48 Psychosis* (Bare Cheek), *The Colleen Bawn* and *This is Our Youth* (Bedrock, Project Arts Centre) and *Anatomy of a Seagull* and *Jesus has my Mom in there* (Loose Canon). Television and film credits includes *Love/Hate*, Winner of the IFTA Actress in a Lead Role Television Award 2013 (Octagon Films), *Happy Valley, The Village, Quirke* and *Ripper Street* (BBC), *Single-Handed* (RTÉ, ITV), *Misfits* (Channel 4), *71* (Warp Films), *Philomena* (Baby Cow Productions) and *Northmen: A Viking Saga* (Elite Films/Salt). Charlie is a graduate of the Gaiety School of Acting, Dublin.

TOM VAUGHAN-LAWLOR
DENNIS

TOM'S PREVIOUS WORK at the Abbey Theatre includes *Juno and the Paycock* (a co-production between the Abbey Theatre and the National Theatre of Great Britain), *The Rivals, The Resistible Rise of Arturo Ui* (Winner of the Irish Times Theatre Award for Best Actor 2008), *Three Sisters, Saved, The School for Scandal* and *The Playboy of the Western World*. Other theatre work includes *Howie the Rookie*, Winner of the Irish Times Theatre Award for Best Actor 2013 (Landmark Productions), *55 Days* (Hampstead Theatre, London), *All My Sons* (West End), *Molly Sweeney* (Leicester Curve), *The Lady from the Sea* (Birmingham Rep), *Henry V,* Ian Charleson Award Commendation (Manchester Royal Exchange), *The Field, The Quare Fellow* (Tricycle

Theatre), *Translations* (National Theatre), *This Lime Tree Bower* (Young Vic), *Philadelphia, Here I Come!* (Gaiety Theatre Dublin). Television and film credits include *Love/ Hate*, Winner of Best Supporting Actor IFTA 2010 and Best Actor 2013 (Octagon Films), *Charlie* (Touchpaper TV/ Element Films), *Foxes, Becoming Jane* and *The Tiger's Tail*. His radio credits include *The Leopard* (BBC Radio 3), *The Serpent, Beguiled Me, In the Real World* (RTÉ Radio). Tom trained at the Royal Academy of Dramatic Art, London.

PAUL WILLS
SET DESIGN

PAUL'S PREVIOUS WORK at the Abbey Theatre includes *Drum Belly*. Other credits include *The Two Gentlemen of Verona* (RSC), *Anna Christie, Making Noise Quietly, The Man Who Had All the Luck, The Cut* (Donmar Warehouse), *Di and Viv and Rose, A Human Being Died That Night* (Hampstead Theatre/ West End), *Routes, The Acid Test, Breathing Corpses* (Royal Court), *The Hypochondriac, A Steady Rain, Home* (Theatre Royal Bath), *My Fair Lady, Afterplay, Blue/Orange* (Sheffield Theatres), *A Number* (Menier Chocolate Factory), *Once A Catholic* (Tricycle Theatre), *Howie The Rookie* (The Barbican and

International Tour), *Dr Faustus, Frontline, The Lightning Child* (Shakespeare's Globe), *Novecento* (Donmar Trafalgar), *The Indian Wants The Bronx* (The Young Vic), *Finding Neverland, Buried Child* (Leicester Curve), *Punk Rock, Blasted, Saved, Secret Theatre, The Chair Plays* (Lyric Hammersmith), *Orpheus Descending, 1984, Macbeth, See How They Run* (Manchester Royal Exchange), *Crestfall* (Theatre 503), *Ben Hur, Little Voice* (Watermill), *Treasure Island, The Second Mrs. Tanqueray* (Rose Theatre Kingston), *Waiting for Godot, Yerma* (West Yorkshire Playhouse), *Serious Money* (Birmingham Rep), *Pornography* (Tricycle/Birmingham Rep/Traverse), *Mammals* (Bush Theatre/UK Tour), *A Kind of Alaska, A Slight Ache* (Gate Theatre), *Prometheus Bound* (New York/The Sound Venue), *The Changeling, Mother Courage and her Children* (ETT). Opera credits include *Intermezzo* (Buxton Opera Festival), *Rusalka* (English Touring Opera), *Sweetness and Badness* (Welsh National Opera) and *The Magic Flute* (National Theatre of Palestine).

PAUL KEOGAN
LIGHTING DESIGN

PAUL'S PREVIOUS WORK at the Abbey Theatre includes *Heartbreak House, The Risen People, Drum Belly* and *No Escape*. Other recent lighting designs include *No Man's Land* and *Firebird* (English National Ballet), *Hansel and Gretel* (Royal Ballet), *Tiny Plays For Ireland 1 and 2* (Fishamble: The New Play Company), *A Tale of Two Cities* (Theatre Royal, Northampton), *Romeo and Juliet, The Hairy Ape, Woyzeck and Plasticine* (Corcadorca), *A Streetcar Named Desire, The Last Summer* and *The Birds* (Gate Theatre), *Big Maggie, Penelope* and *The Walworth Farce* (Druid), *Angel/Babel* (Operating Theatre, Dublin), *Thérèse / La Navarraise, Cristina Regina di Svezia, Snegurochka, The Mines of Sulphur* and *Susannah* (Wexford Festival Opera), *Maria de Buenos Aires* (Cork Opera House), *Lady Macbeth of Mtensk, The Silver Tassie* and *Dead Man Walking* (Opera Ireland), *Mixed Marriage* (Lyric Theatre, Belfast), *Before it Rains* (Sherman Cymru and Bristol Old Vic), *Don Quichotte, Les Dialogues des Carmelites, I Puritani, Eugene Onegin, Idomeneo* and *Pique Dame* (Grange Park Opera), *The Misanthrope* and *A Streetcar Named Desire* (Playhouse, Liverpool), *Semele* (Royal Irish Academy of Music), *La Bohème* and *Wake* (Nationale Reisopera, Netherlands), *Yerma* (West Yorkshire Playhouse), *Novecento* (Trafalgar Studios), *Twelfth Night* and *Intemperance* (Everyman,

Liverpool), *The Taming of the Shrew* (Royal Shakespeare Company), *Harvest* (Royal Court Theatre), *The Stock Da'Wa* (Hampstead Theatre), *Afterplay* and *Blue/Orange* (Crucible Theatre), *Pierrot Lunaire* (Almeida Theatre), *Trad* (Galway Arts Festival), *Man of Aran Re-Imagined* (Once Off Productions), *The Makropulos Case* and *Der Fliegende Holländer* (Opera Zuid, Netherlands) and *Die Zauberflöte* (National Opera of Korea). Paul studied Drama at Trinity College, Dublin and at Glasgow University.

CATHERINE FAY
COSTUME DESIGN

CATHERINE'S PREVIOUS WORK at the Abbey Theatre includes *Aristocrats, Quietly, The Government Inspector, Macbeth, The Playboy of the Western World, Saved, Doubt, Doldrum Bay, Henry IV Part I* (for which she received an Irish Times/ESB Theatre Award nomination), *On Such As We* and *Chair* (Operating Theatre). Recent work includes *Tundra* and *Dogs* (Winner Best Production and Best Design for ABSOLUT Fringe 2012) (Emma Martin Dance), *Ice Child* (Barnstorm Theatre Company), *The Threepenny Opera* (Gate Theatre)

and *Carmen* (Opera Theatre Company). Other work includes *Romeo and Juliet* (joint production with Corcadorca and Cork Opera House), *Body and Forgetting* and *Fast Portraits* (Liz Roche Company). She has designed much of Bedrock's back catalogue including *Wedding Day at the Cro Magnon's, Roberto Zucco, Quay West, Night Just before the Forest, Wideboy Gospel* and *Massacre @ Paris*. Other work includes *It Only Ever Happens in the Movies* (National Youth Theatre), *5 Ways to Drown* (Junk Ensemble), *King Lear* (Second Age Theatre Company), *Mother Goose* and *Beauty and the Beast* (Gaiety Theatre), *Talking to Terrorists* and *Farawayan* (Calypso), *Love and Money, Pyrennes* and *Cruel and Tender* (HATCH Theatre Company), *Adrenalin* (Semper Fi), *Mushroom, The Red Hot Runaways, Antigone* and *Women in Arms* (Storytellers), *Lessness* (Gare St Lazare Players, Kilkenny Arts Festival and National Theatre, London), *Y2K Festival* (Fishamble: The New Play Company) and *Babyjane* (The Corn Exchange). Catherine is a graduate of the National College of Art and Design, Dublin.

PHILIP STEWART
MUSIC

PHILIP'S PREVIOUS WORK at the Abbey Theatre includes *Heartbreak House*, *The Risen People*, *Major Barbara*, *Quietly* (also toured to Edinburgh Festival Fringe 2013), *The House*, *Pygmalion*, *Macbeth*, *Ages of the Moon*, *Lay Me Down Softly*, *Terminus*, *A Number* and *The Big House*. He has contributed music to a broad spectrum of genres including theatre, dance, documentaries and short films. He has been nominated twice for an Irish Times Theatre Award. Philip studied composition at Trinity College Dublin under Donnacha Dennehy and Roger Doyle.

MAISIE LEE
ASSISTANT DIRECTOR

MAISIE IS CURRENTLY Resident Assistant Director at the Abbey Theatre and has worked on *Heartbreak House*, *Aristocrats*, *Twelfth Night*, *Sive* and *The Risen People*. She is Artistic Director of MIRARI productions and has directed all their productions to date, these include *In Dog Years I'm Dead*, Winner of the Stewart Parker Trust Award 2014 (Bewley's Café Theatre and Dublin Fringe Festival 2013), *THRESHOLD* (Turnaround, Project Arts Centre), *When Irish Hearts are Praying* (ABSOLUT Fringe 2011) and *Here Comes Love* (Bewley's Café Theatre). MIRARI Productions are Artists in Residence at Dunamaise Arts Centre, Portlaoise for 2013 - 2014. Other recent work includes Assistant Director to Annabelle Comyn on *The Talk of the Town* (Dublin Theatre Festival 2012), *The Hunt for Red Willie* (Exit Excitedly, Smock Alley Theatre), *BUSK* (Project Arts Centre and Solstice) and *The Tinteán Tales* (Pearse Museum, Rathfarnham). For radio Maisie directed *Moore Than a Garden* and *The Silver Branch* (Dublin South Radio, Alive-O Productions). She is a Drama and Theatre studies graduate of The Samuel Beckett Centre, Trinity College, Dublin.

110th Anniversary Campaign
1904-2014

'In the year of our 110th Anniversary, we would like to thank you for your generous support. Your investment helps us to continue to fuel the flame our founders lit over a century ago: to develop playwrights, support theatre artists and engage citizens throughout Ireland and internationally. Go raibh míle maith agat.'

Fiach Mac Conghail, Director/Stiúrthóir

CORPORATE GUARDIANS

 THE DOYLE COLLECTION

The Westbury Hotel
DUBLIN

The Doyle Collection, official hotel partner of Ireland's national theatre.

 SIPTU

 Ulster Bank

BROWN THOMAS
ESTABLISHED 1849 ADORED EVER SINCE

electric Ireland

McCANN FITZGERALD

 ESB

 Irish Life

DIAGEO
IRELAND

 BEHAVIOUR & ATTITUDES

 AON

ARTHUR COX

 Allianz

 KPMG

Bank of Ireland

 accenture
High performance. Delivered.

 Northern Trust

MEDIA PARTNERS

Sunday Independent

Irish Independent

SUPPORTERS OF PLAYWRIGHT DEVELOPMENT

Deloitte.

CORPORATE AMBASSADORS

Paddy Power
101 Talbot Restaurant
Bewley's
Wynn's Hotel
FCm Travel Solutions
CRH
Conway Communications
The Merrion Hotel
Baker Tilly Ryan Glennon
National Radio Cabs
The Church Bar & Restaurant
Clarion Consulting Limited
Manor House Hotels of Ireland
Zero-G

CORPORATE AMBASSADORS

Irish Poster Advertising
DCC plc
Trocadero
Merrion Capital
Spector Information Security
ely bar & brasserie

CORPORATE PARTNERS

High Performance Training

GUARDIANS OF THE ABBEY

Sen. Fiach Mac Conghail
James McNally

FELLOWS OF THE ABBEY

Frances Britton
Sherril Burrows
Catherine Byrne
The Cielinski Family
Dónall Curtin
Tommy Gibbons
Pamela Fay
James Hickey
Dr. John Keane
Andrew Mackey
Eugene Magee
Gerard & Liv McNaughton
Donal Moore
Pat Moylan
Elizabeth Purcell Cribbin
Marie Rogan & Paul Moore
Sheelagh O'Neill
Mark Ryan

Abbey Theatre
Staff & Supporters

SENIOR MANAGEMENT TEAM

Director / CEO
Senator Fiach Mac Conghail

**Director of Finance
& Administration**
Declan Cantwell

**Director of Public Affairs
& Development**
Oonagh Desire

Literary Director
Aideen Howard

Head of Production
Aisling Mooney

ABBEY THEATRE BOARD OF DIRECTORS

Chairman
Dr. Bryan McMahon (Chairman)
Jane Brennan
Dónall Curtin
Paul Davis
Thomas Kilroy
Deirdre Kinahan
Niamh Lunny
James McNally
Sheelagh O'Neill
Mark Ryan
Paul Smith

 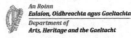

An Roinn
Ealaíon, Oidhreachta agus Gaeltachta
Department of
Arts, Heritage and the Gaeltacht

The Abbey Theatre gratefully acknowledges the financial
support of the Arts Council of Ireland and the support of the
Department of the Arts, Heritage and the Gaeltacht.

Archive partner of the Abbey Theatre.

OUR FEW AND EVIL DAYS

Mark O'Rowe

For James and Michael

Characters

MARGARET, *fifties*
MICHAEL, *fifties, a scar near his eye*
ADELE, *thirty*
DENNIS, *thirties*
GARY, *thirties*

Setting

A large living room/kitchen.

Exit to front hallway and stairs, upstage right. Exit to utility area, upstage left. Windows stage left and stage right.

This text went to press before the end of rehearsals and so may differ slightly from the play as performed.

Prologue

Fade up on MARGARET, *asleep on a sofa bed. It is before dawn. The light is vague, abstract. On a low coffee table beside her sits a glass and a half-full bottle of whiskey.* MICHAEL, *semi-dressed, enters from upstairs, takes the whiskey bottle and glass to the kitchen area, puts the bottle back in the press, rinses the glass at the sink, then goes to the sofa bed and sits down on its edge, touching* MARGARET's *shoulder. She wakes, sits up. They embrace, exchanging several words which we don't hear.* MARGARET *gets off the sofa bed, puts on her dressing gown, and exits upstairs.* MICHAEL *folds the duvet, places it on an armchair. He removes the sheet from the bed, puts it on top of the duvet, takes the pillow, puts it on top of the sheet. He folds the bed away, remaking the sofa, replacing the last couple of cushions. He picks up the duvet cover, sheet and pillow, and exits to the utility area. Hold on the empty room.*

Fade to black.

ACT ONE

Scene One

Early evening. The doorbell rings. MICHAEL *enters from the utility area, then exits to the hallway. We hear the front door open.*

MICHAEL (*offstage*). Hey.

DENNIS (*offstage*). Hey.

MICHAEL (*offstage*). Dennis.

DENNIS (*offstage*). Yeah.

MICHAEL (*offstage*). Good to meet you. Come in.

DENNIS (*offstage*). You too.

> *We hear the front door close.*

MICHAEL (*offstage*). You found us all right.

DENNIS (*offstage*). Yeah.

MICHAEL (*offstage*). In here.

> *As they enter:*

DENNIS. This is odd.

MICHAEL. What? You coming up here?

DENNIS. Yeah.

MICHAEL. I suppose it is a bit.

DENNIS. On my own, like.

MICHAEL. Gimme your jacket, there, and I'll hang it up.

> DENNIS *removes his jacket. As* MICHAEL *takes it and exits again to the hallway:*

I suppose it *is* a bit odd, but probably better here than on your own in the pub all night.

DENNIS. Yeah.

MICHAEL. Or is it?

DENNIS. No, it is, all right.

MICHAEL (*calling up the stairs*). Margaret?

MARGARET (*offstage*). Yeah?

MICHAEL. Dennis is here.

MARGARET (*offstage*). Okay.

MICHAEL (*returning; to* DENNIS). Which one were you in, The Tower?

DENNIS. Which pub?

MICHAEL. Yeah.

DENNIS. Horan's?

MICHAEL. Horan's, and, what, she rang?

DENNIS. Who?

MICHAEL. Belinda.

DENNIS. Oh, is that her name?

MICHAEL. Yeah.

DENNIS. Right. No, Adele didn't say who it was. Just, you know, that a friend of hers needed help or whatever.

MICHAEL. And how long were you sitting there?

DENNIS. An hour? I dunno...

MICHAEL. An hour?!

DENNIS. You mean after she left?

MICHAEL. Uh-huh.

DENNIS. Yeah, about an hour. She rang then and said to come up.

MICHAEL. Right.

DENNIS. Here, like. Said she'd be another while...

MICHAEL. Which she will.

DENNIS.…and that she'd just spoken to you?

MICHAEL. That's right. Which she had. But, listen: we're not gonna let the awkwardness of the situation get to us, are we?

DENNIS. No. Well, we'll do our best not to anyway.

MICHAEL. Exactly. Can I get you a cup of tea?

DENNIS. *Yeah*, sure.

MICHAEL. Or a beer?

DENNIS (*beat*). I'd love a beer, actually.

MICHAEL. Good man. Take a seat there.

> DENNIS *sits down in an armchair as, over the following,* MICHAEL *goes to the kitchen area, takes two bottles of beer out of the fridge and opens them.*

> She's a bit of a pain, to be honest.

DENNIS. Who's that?

MICHAEL. Belinda.

DENNIS. Right.

MICHAEL. Well, she's not, she's fine, but she's one of those people, there's always a bloody *crisis* going on.

DENNIS. Uh-huh.

MICHAEL. You know the type?

DENNIS. I think I do, yeah.

MICHAEL. And she and Adele have that kind of friendship, every time there's a new one, that's who she calls.

DENNIS. Adele is.

MICHAEL. Yeah. And she has to come *running* every time like it's life or death, which, of course, it never actually *is*…

DENNIS. Okay.

MICHAEL.…though you never know, you know? (*Returning.*) And that's the thing, I suppose. It's like the boy and the wolf…

DENNIS. Who cried wolf?

MICHAEL. Huh?

DENNIS. The boy who cried wolf?

MICHAEL. Exactly. (*Giving* DENNIS *his beer.*) …the very time she *does* refuse to come running, that'll be the time it really *is* a crisis, a *real* one…

DENNIS. Right.

MARGARET *enters from upstairs.*

MICHAEL.…like, a *proper* emergency, you know? Anyway…

MARGARET. Hi.

DENNIS (*standing up*). Hello.

MARGARET. Dennis.

DENNIS. Yes.

MARGARET. It's very nice to meet you.

DENNIS (*as they shake hands*). It's very…

MARGARET. I'm Margaret.

DENNIS. Margaret. It's very nice to meet *you*.

MICHAEL. We were discussing Belinda.

MARGARET. Right.

MICHAEL. Do you want a glass of wine?

MARGARET. Eh… yeah.

MICHAEL. White?

MARGARET. No, a glass of red would be lovely, actually. (*To* DENNIS.) Sit down.

She and DENNIS *sit as* MICHAEL *goes to get the wine.*

MICHAEL. I was telling Dennis how needy she can be.

MARGARET. She can.

DENNIS. Okay.

MARGARET. Very needy. Although there are some
advantages… (*To* MICHAEL.) aren't there?

MICHAEL. Are there?

MARGARET. Yeah.

MICHAEL. Like what?

MARGARET. Well, we get to see Adele more often, don't we?
Than if…

MICHAEL. Yeah, I suppose we do.

DENNIS. How's that?

MARGARET. Well, whenever she has to come out to deal with
the latest emergency, she'll usually drop in here for a visit
afterward…

DENNIS. I see.

MARGARET.…try and wind herself down from the stress…
(*To* MICHAEL.) Isn't that right? Oh, thanks.

MICHAEL (*handing her a glass of wine*). You're welcome.

MARGARET (*to* DENNIS).…the drama, you know?

DENNIS. And what are they, childhood friends?

MICHAEL. They are. And…

MARGARET. Well, since secondary school.

MICHAEL. That's right. (*Sitting down.*) And I'm afraid their
relationship is something you'll have to put up with, Dennis,
should, you know, yours continue.

MARGARET. What?

MICHAEL. Which I'm sure it will.

DENNIS. Okay.

MICHAEL. Which I *hope* it will.

MARGARET. And why wouldn't it?

MICHAEL. Well, exactly.

DENNIS (*beat*). No, sure I hope so too.

Silence.

I like your house.

MARGARET. Sorry? Oh...

DENNIS. It's lovely.

MARGARET. Thank you.

DENNIS (*beat*). How long have you lived here?

MICHAEL. Thirty years?

MARGARET. More than *thirty*, Michael.

MICHAEL. I reme... Oh, it *would* be, yeah. I remember
    Margaret crying the night we moved in.

MARGARET. Stop.

DENNIS. Really?

MARGARET. Yeah.

DENNIS. Why were you crying?

MARGARET. Well... it wasn't exactly in the condition it is
    now, Dennis...

DENNIS. Right.

MICHAEL. Far from it.

MARGARET....you know?

MICHAEL. I remember spending weeks, *weeks* now, scraping
    wallpaper off the walls, five, six layers stuck on with, I don't
    know what...

DENNIS. Superglue.

MICHAEL. Yeah, exactly. And filthy!

DENNIS. Really?

MICHAEL. Yeah, the whole house. The people who lived here
    before us...

MARGARET. A couple of brothers.

MICHAEL. That's…

MARGARET. Like, bachelor types?

MICHAEL. That's right. And probably not all there, to be honest, given the mess they left the place in.

MARGARET. Ugh.

DENNIS. Right.

MARGARET. That was the toughest part.

MICHAEL. It was.

MARGARET. The dirt.

MICHAEL. *And* the lack of time we had to clean it up.

MARGARET. That's true.

DENNIS. And why's that?

MARGARET. Hm?

DENNIS. Why did you have so little time?

MARGARET. I was pregnant. Sorry, Dennis.

DENNIS. *Ah*, right.

MICHAEL. Seven months or so.

DENNIS (*to* MARGARET). *Seven?!*

MARGARET. Yeah.

DENNIS. I *see*.

MICHAEL.…you see? Hence…

MARGARET. Exactly.

MICHAEL.…the rush.

DENNIS. And the tears.

MICHAEL. Well, exactly, you know? (*To* MARGARET.) But we did it, didn't we.

MARGARET. What?

MICHAEL. We *got* it ready. (*To* DENNIS.) Or, at least, you know, habitable.

MARGARET. *You* did. (*To* DENNIS.) He's pretending I lifted a finger.

MICHAEL. Ah, you did what you could, now.

Pause.

And so, where do *you* live, Dennis?

DENNIS. Sutton.

MARGARET. Sutton?!

DENNIS. Uh-huh.

MICHAEL. And you go to *Trinity*, do you.

DENNIS. Yeah.

MICHAEL. That's a fairly long way out, is it not?

DENNIS. I suppose it is.

MICHAEL. To commute, like.

DENNIS. Well, with the Dart, though, you see…

MICHAEL. Oh, of course. Do you use it?

DENNIS. Every day.

MICHAEL. …Of course, with the Dart, you're not so bad, I suppose. (*Beat.*) Nice out there…

DENNIS. It is.

MICHAEL. …the coast and all.

MARGARET. Is that why you chose it, Dennis?

DENNIS. Sorry?

MARGARET. Is that why you chose to live out there?

DENNIS. Oh, no…

MARGARET. Right.

DENNIS. …no, sure it wasn't really a choice, to be honest.

MICHAEL. Oh?

DENNIS. Yeah.

MARGARET. Why?

DENNIS. Well, at the time I moved out there, I'd nowhere to stay. It was…

MARGARET. Really?

DENNIS. …it *wasn't*, I mean, a fantastic time in my life.

MARGARET. Oh, I'm sorry to hear that.

MICHAEL. And how long ago was this?

DENNIS. Seven years? Six? Seven?

MICHAEL. Okay.

DENNIS. Anyway. A friend of mine who was living out there offered to put me up for a while. Then, a year or so later, he moved down to Galway, so I stayed on.

MICHAEL. To Galway?

DENNIS. Yeah, he got a job down there, by which time I had a job myself, so I could afford it. I mean…

MARGARET. Afford to stay on.

DENNIS. Exactly. I mean, it's a tiny apartment, now, and I *would* be, probably, better off moving closer to town, but, you know, I'm kind of attached to it now?

MICHAEL. No, I know what you mean. Try living somewhere as long as *we* have, see how attached you become to a place.

DENNIS. Would *you* never move?

MICHAEL. I don't think so. (*To* MARGARET.) Would we?

MARGARET. No.

MICHAEL. Or there'd want to be a very tempting reason.

DENNIS. The Lotto.

MICHAEL. The Lotto might be a good one, yeah.

DENNIS. Get a mansion.

MICHAEL. Even then, though… (*To* MARGARET.) Am I right?

MARGARET....this is home.

DENNIS. Mm-hm.

MARGARET. No, you are. I mean, you can go somewhere nicer, Dennis...

MICHAEL. That's right.

MARGARET....and bigger, but...

DENNIS. No, I know what you mean. It's like...

MARGARET. *Do* you.

DENNIS. Or I can imagine, yeah. It's like, all the life you've lived in a certain place, the experiences...

MARGARET. Exactly.

DENNIS....it's like...

MICHAEL. Well, we raised a family here, you know?

DENNIS. Well, that's what I...

MICHAEL. Sorry. Yes.

DENNIS....what I'm saying. No, that's okay. But I'm sure it *is* like... I dunno, there *must* be a sense, when you move, of leaving all that behind. I mean, even my little place, I have to say... And I know, but...

MARGARET. What?

DENNIS....that it doesn't compare, but I'd genuinely find it... (*His phone is ringing.*) Sorry. (*Reaching into his pocket.*) ...Find it difficult, you know? (*Taking it out and checking the screen.*) It's her. (*Into phone.*) Hello?

MICHAEL. About time.

DENNIS (*pause; into phone*). Okay. (*Pause.*) Okay. Well, I'm here. (*Beat.*) I'm here with your folks. (*Beat.*) No, sure I'm having a beer with them. (*Pause.*) Uh-huh. And so... (*Pause.*) Okay. No, okay, so, we'll see you in a... Cool. See you then. (*Ends the call.*) She's coming now.

MARGARET. Okay. (*Getting up.*) I'll put the food on, so.

MICHAEL. What time is it? (*Looks at his watch.*) Jesus.

MARGARET (*going to the kitchen area*). It's just a bit of lasagne, Dennis. Is that all right?

DENNIS. Yeah, lasagne's great.

MARGARET. Fantastic.

She turns on the oven, takes the lasagne and a couple of bowls of salad, etc., out of the fridge.

DENNIS (*to* MICHAEL). Can I ask you about your scar?

MICHAEL. My scar?

DENNIS. Yeah.

MICHAEL. What do you want to know? How I got it?

DENNIS. Yeah. Well, unless you…

MICHAEL. No, no, no. Not at all. God, that was a *long*, long time ago now. I think I was twenty…?

DENNIS. Right.

MICHAEL. …twenty-one?

DENNIS. And what happened?

MICHAEL. I had a bit of a disagreement with this guy out in Tallaght.

DENNIS. A disagreement.

MICHAEL. Over a girl.

DENNIS. Okay.

MICHAEL. In a pub. You know Tallaght?

DENNIS. Yeah.

MICHAEL. I was chatting her up and it seems they were going out, which I'd no idea about, of course, and the bastard went for me.

DENNIS (*to* MARGARET, *who is now setting the table*). This is before *you* two met, I presume.

MARGARET. Oh, of course.

MICHAEL. Before she tamed me.

MARGARET. Yeah, right.

MICHAEL. So, I got that being thrown against a table, you know, like, against the corner?

DENNIS. Ooh!

MICHAEL. Yeah, I know. I actually thought at the time I was gonna die, the amount of blood that came out. Seventeen stitches, but…

DENNIS. Seven*teen*?!!

MICHAEL. Yeah, but, you ever hear that phrase, 'You should see the other guy'?

DENNIS. Uh-huh.

MICHAEL. Well, you should've seen the prick.

MARGARET. Michael.

MICHAEL. Well, he *was* one.

MARGARET. Fine, but just don't be… (*Sighs.*)

MICHAEL. Cursing?

MARGARET. No.

MICHAEL. What?

MARGARET.…celebrating that stuff.

MICHAEL. I'm not. I'm just answering Dennis's question.

MARGARET. What do you study in Trinity, Dennis?

DENNIS. History and Philosophy.

MARGARET. Really?!

DENNIS. Yeah.

MARGARET. That's impressive.

DENNIS. I'm only in my second *year*, now.

MARGARET. Right.

MICHAEL. Of how many?

DENNIS. Four?

MICHAEL. Well, you're halfway there, then.

DENNIS. Well…

MICHAEL. Sorry, no. Sure the year only starts in September.

DENNIS. Exactly.

MICHAEL. Of course.

MARGARET. And what was it that made you decide to go?

DENNIS. Now?

MARGARET. Hm?

DENNIS. Like, at the age I'm at? Or…

MARGARET. Well, I meant in general, really, but yeah…

The table is now laid. Over the following, she will return to the oven, put the lasagne in and rejoin MICHAEL *and* DENNIS *in the living-room area.*

…I mean, what were you doing before then?

DENNIS. I was an electrician.

MICHAEL. Really? Fully qualified?

DENNIS. *Oh*, yeah.

MICHAEL. Right.

MARGARET. And so, what?

DENNIS (*beat*). What?

MARGARET. What *you*? I mean, how did you come to make such a big decision?

DENNIS. Well… (*Beat.*) Do you really want to know?

MARGARET. Absolutely.

DENNIS. Okay. Well, I realised, I suppose, that all it ever was for me…

MICHAEL. All what ever was?

DENNIS. My job.

MICHAEL. Right.

DENNIS. Sorry… was something I did in the day purely to fund indulging myself at night.

MICHAEL. Going out, like?

DENNIS. Going out…

MICHAEL. Right.

DENNIS. …drinking, all that kind of stuff, but it's like, a couple of years ago, it dawned on me that I was still doing the very same things I was doing when I was twenty, you know? Like the *very* same things, and that really kinda depressed me, because you *do*, you get to the point where, or *I* did anyway, where you think, this isn't enough any more, at least, not to sustain me the rest of my… And I mean in an, I dunno, spiritual, I suppose, way…

MICHAEL. Right.

DENNIS. …the rest of my life, you know?

MICHAEL. That's pretty inspiring, actually.

DENNIS. *I* dunno…

MARGARET. No, it is.

DENNIS. …I mean, I just kind of came to a crossroads, really.

MARGARET. And do you enjoy it?

DENNIS. Ah, yeah, I love it. (*Beat.*) The course? Or…

MARGARET. Yeah.

DENNIS. Oh, absolutely. I mean, it's tough, the whole living thing, you know, managing fees, whatever…

MICHAEL. Is it?

DENNIS. Yeah.

MARGARET. And how do you deal with that?

DENNIS. Work.

MARGARET. Right.

DENNIS. Work my arse off. Excuse me.

MARGARET. That's okay.

MICHAEL. So, where do you work?

DENNIS. Well, I bartend most nights…

MICHAEL. Right.

DENNIS. …do a few hours Saturday, Sunday afternoon. Then there's the odd rewiring job or whatever when I can get it. But, look…

MARGARET. That must be so tough.

DENNIS. Well, it is, but it all depends on how much you want something really, you know?

MICHAEL. That's true.

DENNIS. …I mean, that's another thing I discovered late: if what you want in your life outweighs what you're going to have to put up with to get it…

MICHAEL. Right.

DENNIS. …like, is of more value to you, then it doesn't really warrant, you know…

MICHAEL. Deliberation.

DENNIS. …does it?

MICHAEL. No.

DENNIS. …or uncertainty. Or hesitation. It's a simple choice, and so then, however hard it gets, and it does get hard…

MARGARET. Of course.

DENNIS. …it does, and you do get down, you know, hearted, or whatever, but *when* you do you just have to remind yourself you've already weighed it up…

MICHAEL. Uh-huh.

DENNIS. …and…

MICHAEL....you already know what it's worth it to you.

DENNIS. Exactly. (*Pause*.) Exactly.

MARGARET. That's a nice way of looking at things.

DENNIS. *I* dunno.

MICHAEL. No, it is. It is.

DENNIS. *You* went, though, didn't you?

MICHAEL. Where, to college?

DENNIS. Yeah.

MICHAEL. Do I look like I went to college?

DENNIS. Oh. (*Beat*.) Are you not an engineer? Or...

MICHAEL. I *work* in engineering.

DENNIS. Ah.

MICHAEL. But I never studied for it.

DENNIS. I see. (*Beat; to* MARGARET.) Did you ever go?

MARGARET. To college?

DENNIS. Yeah.

MARGARET (*shakes her head; beat*). It's one of the few things I regret, to be honest.

MICHAEL. Well, it's never too late, as...

DENNIS. True.

MICHAEL....as Dennis has proven.

MARGARET. Yeah, but look at how old he is and look at how old *I* am.

MICHAEL. Still.

MARGARET. What.

DENNIS. Would you want to?

MARGARET (*pause*). No, I don't think so.

DENNIS. Right.

MICHAEL. Adele went...

DENNIS. Yes.

MICHAEL (*to* MARGARET)....which we're pretty proud about, aren't we?

MARGARET. Absolutely.

DENNIS. And her brother?

MARGARET. Sorry?

DENNIS. Did he?

MICHAEL. Her brother?!

DENNIS. Yeah. (*Pause*.) Did Adele not say she had a brother?

MICHAEL. Oh, did she?

DENNIS (*beat*). Why, does she not?

 Black.

Scene Two

MICHAEL, MARGARET, DENNIS *and* ADELE *sit at the kitchen table. They have just finished dinner.*

ADELE....No, she was embarrassed, of course. I mean, given the night that was in it...

MARGARET. Whose night?

ADELE. Mine.

MARGARET. Right.

ADELE. Ours.

MARGARET. You told her you'd a gentleman caller waiting, did you?

DENNIS. A 'gentleman caller'!

MICHAEL. And was it your man?

ADELE. Sure who else would it be?

MARGARET. Her boyfriend, Dennis.

ADELE. Gary.

DENNIS. Okay.

MICHAEL. Now, there's a fella could do with a bit of a hiding.

MARGARET. Michael…

DENNIS. Why, is he bad?

ADELE. Does he *treat* her bad?

DENNIS. Yeah.

ADELE. …Badly, I mean. He does.

MICHAEL. Though she puts up with it.

ADELE. Well, she loves him, Dad. If she loves him, what can you do, you know?

DENNIS. And what does he do?

ADELE. Just treats her like shit. I mean, the stuff he's done to her down through the years, am I right, Mam…?

MARGARET. Mm.

ADELE. …the infidelities…

DENNIS. Right.

ADELE. …the abuses…

DENNIS. Really?

ADELE. Yeah.

DENNIS. What kind of abuses?

ADELE. Well, you name it, really. Running her down…

DENNIS. Insulting her, like?

ADELE. …calling her fat… Yeah, calling her stupid…

MARGARET. In company.

ADELE. Sorry?

MARGARET. In…

ADELE. *Absolutely* in company. Sure you were witness to that once, weren't you?

MARGARET (*to* DENNIS). Horrible.

MICHAEL. Tell him about the money he owes her.

ADELE. Oh, yeah…

MICHAEL (*to* DENNIS). This is mad.

ADELE.…he's owed her fifteen grand for the last five years, which…

DENNIS. Fifteen grand for what?

ADELE. A car he bought, which she's never been able to ask for back.

DENNIS. Why not?

ADELE. Well, in case he might dump her.

DENNIS. You're joking.

ADELE. I'm not. See, the thing she's most terrified of is losing him, which is…

DENNIS. Right.

ADELE.…which…

DENNIS. That's his power.

ADELE. Exactly… which is part of why he feels he can treat her however the hell he likes. And I haven't even given you the half of it, by the way.

MICHAEL. Why, what else is there?

ADELE. Ah, there's other stuff, but, look…

MICHAEL. Like what?

ADELE. Like other stuff. I don't want to get into it. What I'm saying, though, is, I'm sure you can understand how the whole, whatever…

MARGARET. Right.

DENNIS.…situation…

ADELE.…how the whole situation can, yeah, can get her down sometimes, or depressed sometimes, to the point where she really needs someone to talk to, you know?

DENNIS. Mm.

ADELE. Urgently, like. They think it's an act.

MICHAEL. No, we don't.

ADELE.…or, what? An exaggeration?

MARGARET. We just think that maybe she makes too many demands on *you*.

ADELE. She doesn't make *any* demands on me. She calls, that's all…

MARGARET. No, I know, but…

ADELE.…that's it. What I do is my own decision, and yes, I'm there, I'm over there when she needs me, I'm taking care of her. *But: Listen:*

MICHAEL. What?

ADELE.…I don't *have* to go over.

MICHAEL. What do you mean?

ADELE. She doesn't *make* me go over.

MARGARET. And, what about tonight?

ADELE. Well, tonight…

MARGARET.…hm?

ADELE. Well, I'm pretty concerned about her tonight, to be honest.

MARGARET. Why?

ADELE. Well, first… Ah, look…

MARGARET. No, go on.

ADELE.…you don't want to hear this, do you, Dennis?

DENNIS. Of course I do.

ADELE. Are you sure?

MICHAEL. Of course he's sure.

ADELE. You just wanna hear it yourself.

MICHAEL. That's right.

ADELE. All right. Fair enough. Well, first, this is nuts. First, he confessed to her today that he's been seeing another girl on the sly for months now, all right?

MARGARET. Oh, no.

ADELE. And, second… Yeah, and second, he says he's in love with her…

MICHAEL. Right.

ADELE.…like, deeply. And third…

MARGARET. So he's leaving her.

ADELE. No, bec… Belinda?

MARGARET. Yeah.

ADELE. No, because third… You're not gonna believe this, Mam. Third, he told her he wouldn't as long as she understands that he's with this woman as well…

DENNIS. The other one.

ADELE. Yes.

MICHAEL. That he's with the both of them.

ADELE.…and that he can come and go between the two as he pleases.

DENNIS. God.

MICHAEL. And did she…?

ADELE. I know. (*To* MICHAEL.) And did she agree to it?

MICHAEL. Yeah.

ADELE. She did.

MICHAEL. Ah, for Jaysus' sake.

ADELE (*on 'sake'*). She has. Or, at least, for the *moment* she has. But she's devastated, and I mean, really…

MARGARET. Right.

ADELE.…like, scary upset. Like, worryingly, you know? Like, at least, whatever shit she had to suffer before…

MARGARET. That's right.

ADELE.…at least he was *hers*. But *now*…

DENNIS. Uh-huh.

ADELE.…she has to share him…?!

MICHAEL. Right.

ADELE.…with some *other* bitch?! And so…

MARGARET. Mm.

ADELE. And so now I think she's suddenly facing the possibility that this, you know, might be the end…

MARGARET. Okay.

DENNIS. 'The end' meaning what…?

ADELE. Well…

DENNIS.…him leaving her?

ADELE. Yeah, or them breaking up in general, like. Because she's incapable, she says… and, I have to say, I believe her…

MARGARET.…of putting up with it.

ADELE. Yeah.

MICHAEL. Well, good for her.

ADELE.…which is why… Well, we'll see about that, you know? But, which is why I had to go over and…

DENNIS. Right. Because…

ADELE. Yeah, and comfort her tonight, because it was, you know, a far bigger crisis than usual. (*Pause*.) And because she was far more *upset* than usual.

MICHAEL. Mm.

　　Pause.

DENNIS. I can never understand how a person can treat another person like that.

MICHAEL. Or allow themself to.

ADELE. Huh?

MICHAEL. Or allow themself to be treated like that.

MARGARET. But you *do*.

MICHAEL. What?

MARGARET. You *do* understand. She loves him, Michael.

MICHAEL. Yeah, but…

MARGARET. I mean, if she loves him, Adele, sure, said it herself, then what choice does she have? It's not her fault he's a… (*To* ADELE.) What is he?

ADELE. I don't know.

MARGARET. An asshole?

ADELE. Worse than an *ass*hole, Mam.

MARGARET (*to* MICHAEL). It's not her fault she's in love with a guy like that, but she is in love, so you can't expect, really, rhyme or reason out of her…

DENNIS. True.

MARGARET.…or common sense, you know?

DENNIS. It's luck.

MARGARET. Hm?

DENNIS. It's a matter of luck, really, isn't it? Who you happen to fall for.

MARGARET. Yeah, I suppose it is. (*Beat*.) Anyway… (*Getting up*.) So no coffee.

DENNIS. No, honestly.

MICHAEL. No.

MARGARET. Okay.

She begins clearing the table.

ADELE. That was delicious, Mam.

DENNIS. Can I give you a hand?

MARGARET. Don't be stupid.

MICHAEL. It was.

ADELE. Hm?

MICHAEL. No, I'm just saying, it *was* delicious.

DENNIS. It was.

MARGARET. Well, I'm glad.

She continues to clear the table. After several moments:

MICHAEL. So, how long are you two actually going out?

DENNIS. About a month.

MICHAEL. Oh, is that all?

DENNIS. Isn't it?

ADELE. Yeah, about that.

MARGARET. And how did you meet?

DENNIS. Did Adele not tell you?

MICHAEL. Adele tells us very little, Dennis.

ADELE. Give me a break.

MICHAEL. Well, you do.

ADELE. I tell you lots of things.

MICHAEL. Like what?

ADELE. *I* dunno.

MICHAEL. Like what?

ADELE. Like about Belinda. Sure have we not been…?

MARGARET. Yeah, but about your*self*, Adele.

ADELE. Well…

MARGARET. About your life.

ADELE. Well, I'm… *I* don't know…

DENNIS. You're private.

ADELE. Yes.

DENNIS. I've noticed that myself, actually.

MARGARET. Have you, Dennis?

DENNIS. Or reticent.

MICHAEL. Right.

ADELE. Well, that's how I am, you know? Information is given only on a need-to-know basis.

MICHAEL. Is that right?

ADELE. Yeah.

MARGARET. 'Need-to-know basis'!

MICHAEL. Well, she likes you anyway, Dennis.

DENNIS. Really?

MICHAEL. Ah, yeah.

DENNIS. How do you know?

MICHAEL. Well, it's seldom she'd ever bring *any*one out to meet us.

ADELE. Dad!

MICHAEL. Isn't it, Margaret?

MARGARET. Like, a boyfriend?

MICHAEL. Yeah.

MARGARET. Oh, absolutely.

MICHAEL.…And even when she *has* done, it'd be, like, six months…?

DENNIS. Really?

MICHAEL.…into the, yeah, the relationship…

DENNIS. Right.

MICHAEL.…or a year?

ADELE. No, it wouldn't.

MICHAEL. Well, maybe not *that* long, no. A month is fast, though.

DENNIS. Well…

MARGARET. It is.

DENNIS.…I don't know what to say. (*Beat; to* ADELE.) I'm honoured.

MICHAEL. So, go on.

DENNIS. What.

MICHAEL. Tell us how you met.

DENNIS. How we met.

MICHAEL. Unless it's embarrassing, is it?

DENNIS. No, not at all.

MICHAEL. So…

MARGARET. Why don't you move over there to the comfy seats?

MICHAEL (*to* ADELE *and* DENNIS). Will we move over here to the comfy seats?

ADELE. Yeah, sure, why not?

MARGARET. Bring your glasses with you.

As they move to the living-room area and sit:

MICHAEL. So, go on.

DENNIS. Well, it was in Mulligan's… (*To* ADELE.) wasn't it?

ADELE. Yeah.

DENNIS.…And Adele was there with…

MICHAEL. On Poolbeg Street.

ADELE. That's right.

MICHAEL. That's a great little pub. Go on. Sorry.

MARGARET (*to* ADELE). Who were you there with?

ADELE. Niamh…

MARGARET. Uh-huh.

ADELE.…a couple of others; Emma from work, Suzy… It was Suzy's birthday, actually.

MICHAEL. And…?

ADELE (*to* DENNIS). Go on.

MICHAEL. *You* go on.

ADELE. But I'm the one who never tells anyone *any*thing, Dad.

MARGARET. Ah, go on, Adele!

ADELE. All right. Well, this guy appears and asks if he can speak to me for a moment…

MARGARET. Dennis.

ADELE. Yeah.

MARGARET. Right.

ADELE.…like, out of the blue…

MICHAEL (*to* DENNIS). And who were *you* with?

DENNIS. I was there on my own. (*To* ADELE.) Actually, this *is* fairly embarrassing.

MICHAEL. No it's not.

ADELE. Do you want me to stop?

DENNIS (*beat*). No, sure go on.

MICHAEL. Good man.

ADELE.… 'Can I speak to you for a moment?' and everyone's like, 'Which one of us is he talking to?' Emma assuming, of course, it's her, the cow; Suzy the same…

DENNIS. Why assuming?

ADELE. Well, usually if someone in that particular group is approached in that way, it's one of them.

MARGARET. Really?

ADELE. Yeah.

MARGARET. I don't get that at all.

MICHAEL. All right, so, 'Can I speak to you?'

ADELE. Yeah, and it's me it turns out he's talking to. So I say, 'Fine…'

MICHAEL. Uh-huh.

ADELE. '…Why not?' and he takes me aside and, very matter-of-factly – very *politely*, actually, also – tells me I'm beautiful, don't you? 'I think you're beautiful…'

MICHAEL. Very smooth…

DENNIS. Yeah, right.

MICHAEL (*to* MARGARET).…do you hear this?

MARGARET. Yeah.

ADELE.…and he asks for my number, which, since he does it so timidly…

MICHAEL. Was he timid?!

ADELE. He was.

DENNIS. No, I wasn't.

MARGARET.…You gave him it.

ADELE. Yes. (*To* DENNIS.) You were.

DENNIS. I thought I was *very* self-assured.

ADELE. You were timid. I loved that about you. It's *why* I decided to give you it.

MARGARET. And were they disgusted?

ADELE. Who? Oh…

MARGARET. Emma and…

ADELE. No, they were happy for me, actually.

MARGARET. Really!

ADELE (*beat*). In a condescending kind of way.

MARGARET. The bitches. God forgive me.

MICHAEL. And were you on your own there, Dennis?

DENNIS. In Mulligan's?

MICHAEL. Yeah.

DENNIS. I was, yeah. I'd actually only finished up for the day, and I didn't have work myself that night, so...

MICHAEL. Right.

DENNIS. ...that kind of situation, rare as it is these days, I have to say, I might get a paper and go for a quiet pint before I head for the Dart. I think that night I stayed for a couple, though, which, I suppose, was lucky given...

MICHAEL. Of course.

DENNIS. ...who walked in the door. But that thing, that approaching a girl, that getting her number, isn't something I'd normally...

MICHAEL. Yeah, right.

DENNIS. ...normally do. No, really, like, ever, and *yeah*, her friends were attractive... There were *plenty* of good-looking girls there, actually...

MARGARET. Right.

DENNIS. ...but Adele was more, I dunno... on top of her looks, by the way, which, I'd say, were the equal of *any* of theirs...

MARGARET. Oh, so would I.

DENNIS. ...*Easily*.

ADELE. You're so good.

MARGARET. More what?

DENNIS. Sorry?

MARGARET. Adele was more what?

DENNIS. More real, I suppose.

MARGARET. More real.

DENNIS....Or *herself*.

MICHAEL. So, she gave you her number...

MARGARET. That's lovely, actually.

DENNIS....gave me her number, I called her the following night...

MICHAEL. Couldn't wait.

DENNIS. I couldn't.

ADELE. I couldn't wait myself, to be honest. I was thrilled when he did.

DENNIS....and then, the night after that, we went out...

MICHAEL. Where'd you go?

ADELE. Just for drinks. Just O'Donoghue's.

MARGARET. Right.

ADELE....and that was that. We obviously liked each other enough, we're here now, doing the parent thing.

MICHAEL....'Meeting the parents'. I hope it hasn't been *too* traumatic.

DENNIS. Not at all. It's been great. (*To* MARGARET.) And the lasagne really was lovely.

MARGARET. Thank you.

MICHAEL. Late as we ate.

ADELE. I'm sorry...

MARGARET. Michael...

MICHAEL. I'm teasing her, for God's sake! (*Beat.*) And has *she* met *your* parents yet, Dennis? (*Pause.*) Or...

ADELE. Dad...

DENNIS (*to* MICHAEL). You've just done what I did earlier.

ADELE....Dennis's parents are dead.

MICHAEL. Oh, shit.

DENNIS. That's okay.

MARGARET. Oh, no! Oh, Dennis!

DENNIS. Don't worry about it. They're gone a while now, actually.

ADELE (*to* DENNIS). What did you do?

MARGARET. Still…

DENNIS (*to* ADELE). Huh?

ADELE. Earlier.

MICHAEL. No, we just… Dennis asked if Jonathan went to college.

ADELE. Jonathan?!

MICHAEL. Yeah.

ADELE (*to* DENNIS). How do you know about Jonathan?

DENNIS (*beat*). Well, you mentioned him once, and I thought…

ADELE. I mentioned him once?!

DENNIS. Yeah.

ADELE. Did I?

DENNIS. You said you used to… Did you not say once that, when you were kids, you used to go to Cork, or…

MICHAEL. West Cork.

DENNIS. Right.

ADELE. We did.

DENNIS. …and fish for crabs?

MARGARET. Do you *remember* that, Adele?!

ADELE. I do, yeah.

MICHAEL. Baltimore.

MARGARET. That's right. We used to use rashers to catch them. God, that was…

MICHAEL. Mm.

MARGARET....so long ago, wasn't it?

MICHAEL. Happy days.

MARGARET. They were.

ADELE. And so, what, you discussed what happened to him, and...?

MICHAEL. Jonathan.

ADELE. Yeah.

MICHAEL. We did. Well, we told him the situation, since he'd...

DENNIS....since I'd put my foot in it.

MICHAEL. Listen...

MARGARET. No, you didn't.

MICHAEL....Just like we just did regarding your parents.

ADELE (*to* DENNIS). Sorry I hadn't...

DENNIS. That's okay.

ADELE....hadn't told you. I just...

DENNIS. That's fine. No, that's something, God, I mean...

MARGARET. Yes.

DENNIS....that's something anyone would have a problem telling...

MICHAEL....let alone Adele.

ADELE. Very funny.

DENNIS. No, but I mean until they'd gotten to a point where they felt they trusted the other person enough to...

MICHAEL (*to* ADELE). And do you, Adele?

ADELE. What?

MICHAEL. Trust him enough. Given we've kind of jumped the gun on you.

ADELE (*beat*). Yes.

MICHAEL. All right, then.

ADELE. I do.

DENNIS. Well, I'm very glad you do.

MARGARET. And when did they die, Dennis?

DENNIS (*beat*). My parents?

MARGARET. Or is that a very nosy question?

DENNIS. No, not at all. My dad was when I was young, of…

MARGARET. Right.

DENNIS.…of a heart attack. I barely remember him. And my
    mother was about seven years ago…

MARGARET. Right.

DENNIS.…That was cancer.

MARGARET. God…

MICHAEL. What kind?

DENNIS. Ovarian.

MARGARET.…That's so terrible!

ADELE. Dennis took care of her at the…

MICHAEL. Really?

ADELE.…yeah, at the end.

DENNIS. Well, *near* the end.

MARGARET. On your own?

DENNIS. For a while, yeah.

MARGARET. Right.

DENNIS. There was only me around at the time, you see, so…

ADELE. Shit.

   Her phone is ringing. She takes it out, checks it.

   Sorry.

MICHAEL. Who is it?

ADELE (*answering it*). Hello?

MICHAEL. Adele.

ADELE (*getting up; into phone*). No, no, you're all right. What *is* it…? (*Pause.*) Uh-huh…

She exits to the utility area.

MICHAEL. I bet it's bloody Belinda.

ADELE (*offstage, into phone*).…Okay. And…

We hear the back door open.

No, go on…

We hear it close.

MICHAEL. Pain in the arse. (*To* MARGARET.) Will I open another bottle?

MARGARET. Yeah, if you want.

MICHAEL (*getting up*). Would you like another glass, Dennis?

DENNIS. Eh… *yeah*, sure…

MICHAEL. Or a beer?

DENNIS. No, sure I'll stick with the wine if that's okay.

MICHAEL. Cool.

He goes to get it. After a moment:

MARGARET. And how long did you take care of her, Dennis?

DENNIS. My mother?

MARGARET. Yeah.

DENNIS. Not long. A few months.

MARGARET. Okay.

DENNIS. My sisters kind of took over then.

MICHAEL (*returning with a bottle of wine*). Your sisters.

DENNIS. Yeah, well, both of them live in Australia, see, so, when she was nearer to the end, they came home and kind of relieved me of most of the burden.

MARGARET. Right. Oh, well, *that's* good.

DENNIS. Mm.

MARGARET. I'd say you were glad of the help, were you?

We hear the back door open. Beat.

DENNIS. Sorry?

We hear the back door close.

MARGARET. I said, I'd say you were glad of the help.

ADELE (*entering*). I have to go over. I'm sorry.

MICHAEL. What?!

MARGARET. You're joking!

ADELE. No.

MICHAEL. You can't go over.

ADELE (*exiting to hallway*). I'm sorry!

MICHAEL. This…

MARGARET. Ah, Adele!

MICHAEL.…This is an important night.

ADELE (*offstage*). I know it's important, Dad, it's important to me… (*Re-entering; putting her coat on.*) But if you knew what kind of state she's in… I'm sorry, Dennis.

MARGARET. What kind of state is she in?

ADELE. Suicidal?

MICHAEL. Give me a break.

ADELE. I'm telling you, Dad. I've never heard her like this before. She's hysterical.

DENNIS. Is she?

ADELE. Yeah, I mean…

MARGARET. God.

ADELE.…the very idea of what he's doing…

MICHAEL. What Gary's doing.

ADELE. Yes... is...

DENNIS. Right.

ADELE....is... (*Beat.*) I'm telling you, Dennis, is just...

DENNIS. She's bad.

ADELE. She is.

DENNIS. All right. Well, if you need to *go*, then...

ADELE. I do, but I need you to understand that this happening doesn't mean I don't take this...

DENNIS. Right.

ADELE....seriously.

MICHAEL. Oh, we do understand, Adele. We just don't like it. (*To* DENNIS.) Do we?

ADELE (*to* DENNIS). I don't either, but...

DENNIS. I know.

ADELE....she needs me.

DENNIS. Go if you need to go.

ADELE. Are you sure?

DENNIS. Yes.

ADELE. Thanks for being, thanks so much...

DENNIS. Uh-huh.

ADELE....for being so understanding.

She kisses him.

MARGARET. How long do you reckon you'll be?

ADELE. An hour? (*To* DENNIS.) Will you be okay to wait?

DENNIS. Uh... yeah...

MARGARET. Do you know what time it is, Adele?

ADELE. I know. I'll be back in an hour.

MARGARET. All right.

ADELE. Bye.

MARGARET. Bye.

MICHAEL. Bye.

DENNIS. Bye.

She exits to the hall. We hear the front door open and close.
Silence.

MICHAEL. Jesus.

MARGARET. Yeah.

MICHAEL. So…

DENNIS. Mm.

MICHAEL.…here we are again.

DENNIS (*pause*). What do you mean?

MICHAEL. Just the three of us, like.

DENNIS. Oh, right. You know what? Maybe I *should* go,
    should I?

MICHAEL. What?!

MARGARET. Why?

DENNIS. Well, it's late, like you said, or *getting* late, and…

MICHAEL. Don't be silly.

DENNIS. I just… I hate to be, like…

MICHAEL. What? An imposition?

DENNIS. Yeah.

MICHAEL. You're not, Dennis. Seriously.

MARGARET. Sit down, Dennis.

    MICHAEL *opens the bottle of wine, begins filling their*
    glasses.

MICHAEL. It's been great to meet you.

MARGARET. It has.

DENNIS. Well, it's been great to meet *you*.

MICHAEL. You're a… Jesus, if I can say this now, without
    coming across as, whatever… disingenuous…

DENNIS. Right.

MICHAEL.…you seem like a very decent fella.

DENNIS. Okay.

MICHAEL. Impressive, I'd even say. (*To* MARGARET.) Doesn't he?

MARGARET. Absolutely.

MICHAEL. Well, thank you.

MICHAEL. And patient.

DENNIS. Sorry?

MICHAEL. You seem very patient as well, and I'll tell you something you maybe already know: that's a crucial quality to have if you're dealing with Adele. (*To* MARGARET.) Right?

MARGARET. Mm.

MICHAEL. Forbearance.

DENNIS. I think I *do* already know.

MICHAEL. Or you're finding out. Am I right?

MARGARET. Michael…

MICHAEL. I'm messing.

MARGARET. Adele is a wonderful girl, Dennis.

DENNIS. I know.

MARGARET. A sensitive…

MICHAEL. Yes.

MARGARET.…a caring… (*To* MICHAEL.) Isn't she?

MICHAEL. Oh, abso*lute*ly.

DENNIS. No, I'm very aware of that. (*Beat*.) I'm *very* aware. She's amazing.

Pause.

MICHAEL. All right, so, will we do a toast?

DENNIS. Yeah.

MICHAEL. What'll we toast to?

MARGARET. Dennis?

DENNIS. What?

MARGARET. You're the guest.

DENNIS. Oh, right. So *I've* to make it, do I?

MARGARET. Well, if you want.

DENNIS. No, okay. Em…

> *Silence.*

> Sorry, let me think for a second.

> *Another silence.*

> *Black.*

Scene Three

Much later that night. The room is empty. MARGARET enters from the utility area, carrying sheet, duvet and pillow. She opens the sofa bed and makes it up. She goes to the kitchen area, gets a bottle of whiskey from the press, sits down at the table and pours herself a glass. She takes a sip. Silence. DENNIS enters from upstairs.

DENNIS. Hi.

MARGARET. Hi.

DENNIS. I'm sorry, I just… I wanted to get a glass of water?

MARGARET. Yeah, go ahead.

DENNIS (*going to the sink*). I didn't think there was anyone still down here.

> *He fills a glass, drinks half of it, then turns back to* MARGARET. *Beat. Of the sofa bed:*

> Is that for you?

MARGARET. The bed?

DENNIS. Yeah.

MARGARET. It is.

DENNIS (*beat*). It isn't because of me, though, is it?

MARGARET. Oh, no, not at all. (*Beat.*) I have trouble sleeping, you see, so...

DENNIS. Really?

MARGARET. Yeah, so I like to stay down here, so that, if I want, I can get a cup of tea for myself, or a glass of whiskey, or watch TV without, you know, worrying about Michael.

DENNIS. Worrying?

MARGARET. About disturbing him.

DENNIS. Right. (*Pause; he finishes the water.*) Anyway. Sorry to bother you.

MARGARET. That's okay.

He rinses the glass, puts it on the draining board. Then, heading for the stairs:

DENNIS. I'll see you.

MARGARET. Night, Dennis.

DENNIS. Actually... (*Stops, turns back.*) Can I ask you something?

MARGARET. Sure.

DENNIS....While I have you alone. Do you mind?

MARGARET. Not at all. About Adele, is it?

DENNIS. Yeah. Well, kind of. It's slightly complicated, actually.

MARGARET. Really?

DENNIS. Yeah.

MARGARET. Sit down there, so.

DENNIS. Are you sure?

MARGARET. Well, yeah, if it's going to *take* a minute... Is it?

DENNIS. Probably, yeah.

MARGARET. Sit down, so.

As he does:

By the way, I'm really sorry about all this.

DENNIS. All what?

MARGARET. Belinda...

DENNIS. Right.

MARGARET. ...Adele not coming home...

DENNIS. That's fine. Although it does kinda feel a bit odd still being here.

MARGARET. Without her.

DENNIS. Yeah.

MARGARET. No, I know, but there was no way Michael was going to let you go, Dennis.

DENNIS. No, I got that.

MARGARET. ...you know?

DENNIS. And, look: if she felt the situation necessitated her staying over, then...

MARGARET. No, of course. I just...

DENNIS. What?

MARGARET. ...I'd hate to think you thought she didn't... respect you or that she was taking you for granted...

DENNIS. I know she's not taking me for granted.

MARGARET. Cos that's not Adele.

DENNIS. I know it's not, sure I know *Adele*, you know?

MARGARET. So, what do you want to ask me?

DENNIS. Can I make an observation first?

MARGARET. An observation?

DENNIS. Yeah.

MARGARET. Okay.

DENNIS (*pause*). It's really tough on you, isn't it.

MARGARET. What?

DENNIS. Your son.

MARGARET. My son?

DENNIS. Yeah.

MARGARET. Where the hell did that come out of?

DENNIS. I don't know. It's just, you're so…

MARGARET. What?

DENNIS. …*sad*, so…

MARGARET. Am I?

DENNIS. Yeah. I mean, even when you're laughing.

MARGARET (*beat*). What the hell are you talking about?

DENNIS. Has nobody ever said that to you?

MARGARET. No.

DENNIS. Ah, they have…

MARGARET. Well…

DENNIS. …surely. I mean, you just… you *do* have the air about you of someone… (*Beat*.) someone suffering under some awful weight, someone…

MARGARET. Right.

DENNIS. …someone grieving, I suppose. (*Pause*.) How old was he?

MARGARET. He was eleven.

DENNIS. And why did he do it?

Pause.

Sorry.

MARGARET. No, that's okay.

DENNIS. I…

MARGARET. That's fine, Dennis, no. I just… (*Beat.*) We actually don't *know* why.

DENNIS. Okay.

MARGARET. It was something he threatened fairly often, or at least whenever Michael and I were angry at him…

DENNIS. Right.

MARGARET.…which *was* fairly often.

DENNIS. What do you mean by 'threatened'?

MARGARET. I don't know. He'd tell us, 'I'll run away and someone'll get me, someone awful, and *do* things to me. Horrible things,' he'd say…

DENNIS. Right.

MARGARET.… 'terrible things.' And, of course, he was probably right because that's what someone probably did.

DENNIS (*beat*). Mm.

MARGARET. It's *likely* that's what somebody did, you know?

DENNIS. You don't really know that for sure, though, do you?

MARGARET. No, but a child runs away from home, an eleven-year-old, Dennis, and nobody sees him, and all the investigating and all the searches and all the help from everybody – and there *was*, there was plenty. People were *so* good, really – and nothing…

DENNIS. Right.

MARGARET.…Not a trace. I mean, that's what one fellow told me, this detective…

DENNIS. What did he tell you?

MARGARET. Well, he said that, a child that age, the odds that he could evade all that all by himself…

DENNIS. Uh-huh.

MARGARET.…were miniscule. Whereas…

DENNIS. Right.

MARGARET....like, infinitesimal, really, you know? Whereas the alternative...

DENNIS. Mm. (*Beat*.) No, I get you.

Long pause.

And was he a bad kid?

MARGARET (*beat*). What do you mean?

DENNIS. No, just, you were saying that you were often angry at him.

MARGARET. We were.

DENNIS. And, so...

MARGARET. He had problems, though, Dennis. He wasn't 'bad'.

DENNIS. I see.

MARGARET. But...

DENNIS. Sorry.

MARGARET. No, that's all right. But, yes. I can't deny he was often extremely difficult...

DENNIS. Right.

MARGARET....you know?

DENNIS. In what way?

MARGARET. In what way?

DENNIS. Yeah.

MARGARET (*pause*). He could be very destructive.

DENNIS. Could he?

MARGARET. Yeah, or malicious. I mean, there were things he did, I have to say, that were pretty awful.

DENNIS. Like what?

MARGARET. Ah, nothing.

DENNIS. Okay.

MARGARET. This and that. It's not really worth getting into. (*Pause*.) But afterwards, then, he'd often be so upset...

DENNIS. Really?

MARGARET.... Yeah, and frustrated with himself. He told me once... You know, like, I'd sometimes ask him why he did it...

DENNIS. Did what?

MARGARET. Acted the way he did. Because he was often good as well, Dennis...

DENNIS. Right.

MARGARET.... and funny...

DENNIS. Was he?

MARGARET. Oh, absolutely... and full of love and, *I* don't know... Why am I telling you all this?

DENNIS. Why? Well...

MARGARET. Yeah.

DENNIS. Well, because I asked.

MARGARET. You didn't ask for a monologue, though, did you?

DENNIS. No.

MARGARET (*looking up at the clock*). What time is it anyway?

DENNIS (*on 'anyway'*). Although Adele thinks I have that kind of personality...

MARGARET. What kind?

DENNIS.... that people like to confide in me?

MARGARET. Right...

DENNIS. Not *her*, now.

MARGARET. But other people.

DENNIS. Exactly.

MARGARET (*beat*). Ah, no, now, I think maybe she *is* a bit more open than normal when you're around.

DENNIS. Is she?

MARGARET. Yeah.

DENNIS. Well, there you go.

MARGARET. There you go indeed.

DENNIS. But, go on.

MARGARET. What.

DENNIS. You were saying you'd ask him why he did what he
    did.

MARGARET. I would, yeah.

DENNIS. And what would *he* say?

MARGARET (*pause*). He'd say he could feel there was
    something missing in him…

DENNIS. What do you mean?

MARGARET.…inside him, that he felt wasn't missing with
    other kids.

DENNIS. And what was that?

MARGARET. He didn't know.

DENNIS. Okay.

MARGARET. But he said he felt it a lot.

DENNIS. This absence.

MARGARET. Sorry?

DENNIS. This…

MARGARET. Exactly…

DENNIS. Right.

MARGARET.…Exactly. This absence. And it hurt, he said, and
    because it hurt, and because he wasn't able, you know, to
    even figure out what it was, that made him really, whatever…

DENNIS. Angry.

MARGARET....angry, yeah. Confused. I mean, and we should have brought him to someone, of course, a therapist, something like that... And there's *another* thing to feel guilty about, but we didn't.

DENNIS. Right.

MARGARET. We didn't. And who knows if it would've done any good in any case, you know?

Long pause.

He used to call me 'Mammy.' (*Beat.*) You'd hear all the other kids, 'Mam...'

DENNIS. Uh-huh.

MARGARET....or, 'Mom', or, Jesus, 'Mum'...

DENNIS. What did Adele say?

MARGARET. Adele said, 'Mam'...

DENNIS. Okay.

MARGARET....*says*, Mam, but, yeah... (*Beat.*) with him it was always 'Mammy'.

Silence.

DENNIS. I'm sorry.

MARGARET (*on 'sorry'*). But it isn't grief I feel, Dennis.

DENNIS. Okay.

MARGARET....It's worse than grief.

DENNIS. Cos you never know.

MARGARET. Hm?

DENNIS. I said, cos you never know.

MARGARET. That's right.

DENNIS. It never ends. No, I get that now. And...

MARGARET. 'Now'?

DENNIS. Huh?

MARGARET (*beat*). You get it now?

DENNIS. Well, cos I didn't before, you know?

MARGARET. Before what?

DENNIS. Tonight.

MARGARET. Right.

DENNIS. And…

MARGARET. But we never met before tonight.

DENNIS. Well, we did, actually. (*Beat.*) We did. I used to see you on Saturday afternoons, you'd come into O'Neill's about half two or three and have, am I right…? a cup of coffee, and sit, am I right…?

MARGARET. You are.

DENNIS. …for about an hour and a half, and stare, and I'd think, 'What the hell is wrong with her?' Because I could see it…

MARGARET. You worked there?

DENNIS. You don't remember me?

MARGARET. No.

DENNIS. I bet you do, but hang on…

MARGARET. I do?

DENNIS. I bet you do, but I'm saying, you'd stare and, I swear, that terrible sadness came off you even then. It was tangible.

MARGARET. Tangible.

DENNIS. Yeah, sure it's tangible now.

MARGARET. I don't believe it!

DENNIS (*beat*). Mad, huh?

MARGARET. When did you realise this?

DENNIS. Tonight…

MARGARET. And…

DENNIS. …as soon as I saw you.

MARGARET. …And why didn't you say anything?

DENNIS. I don't know. I thought it might have been…

MARGARET (*beat*)….weird.

DENNIS. Yeah.

MARGARET. Mm. (*Beat.*) It probably would've. And, so…

DENNIS (*on 'so'*). And…

MARGARET. Sorry.

DENNIS. No, sure go on.

MARGARET. And, so what do you mean by you bet I do?

DENNIS. What do you mean?

MARGARET. You said you bet I *do* remember you.

DENNIS. Oh, yeah. Well, do you not remember the day you
   burst into tears?

MARGARET (*pause*). In O'Neill's?! Oh, I do!

DENNIS. And a barman comforted you?

MARGARET. Oh, you're joking!

DENNIS. No.

MARGARET. Of course I remember. (*Beat.*) Oh, my God!
   Dennis! You were so understanding! I don't believe this!
   Actually, you know what? I knew there something familiar
   about you. You told me…

DENNIS. What?

MARGARET. Huh?

DENNIS. What did I tell you?

MARGARET. You said it would pass.

DENNIS. That's right.

MARGARET. Whatever it was would pass. How long ago was
   this? You were lovely.

DENNIS. A year and half?

MARGARET. Is that how long?

DENNIS. And you never came in again.

MARGARET. I didn't. No.

DENNIS. Why not?

MARGARET. I couldn't. I'd made such a fool of myself.

DENNIS. No, you hadn't.

MARGARET. I had. There's no way I could've gone back in there, having embarrassed myself like that.

DENNIS. And why were you crying?

MARGARET. We've just been talking about it.

DENNIS. Jonathan.

MARGARET. Right. You get phases...

DENNIS. Even now.

MARGARET. ...even now, where it all becomes very hard to deal with. They come and go...

DENNIS. ...but that was a bad one.

MARGARET. That was a bad one, yeah.

DENNIS (*pause*). So it *hasn't* passed.

MARGARET. Well, it's never *going* to, Dennis, no. (*Beat.*) But it was so generous of you to...

DENNIS. Right.

MARGARET. ...to come over and to suggest that it would.

   Silence.

DENNIS. I actually saw you one other time after that.

MARGARET. You're kidding. When?

DENNIS. A few months ago?

MARGARET. Where? This is crazy.

DENNIS. Brown Thomas.

MARGARET. You should've said hello. Or maybe not.

DENNIS. I did.

MARGARET. You did?

DENNIS. I said 'Hi,' but you just walked past.

MARGARET (*beat*). I'm sorry, Dennis.

DENNIS. That's okay.

MARGARET. Was I on my own?

DENNIS. No.

MARGARET. Who was I with?

DENNIS. Adele.

MARGARET. Adele?! (*Pause.*) So, you'd seen her before.

DENNIS. Before what?

MARGARET. Before you met her in Mulligan's.

DENNIS. Yes.

MARGARET. That's odd.

DENNIS. Well, that's kind of why, you see, I went after her.

MARGARET. What do you mean?

DENNIS. Like, approached her.

MARGARET. Why?

DENNIS. Because I'd seen her with you.

MARGARET (*beat*). I'm not…

DENNIS. Can I just say something and ask you not to panic?

MARGARET. To panic?

DENNIS. Yeah.

MARGARET (*half-joking*). You're not in love with me or
     something, are you?

     Long pause.

     Oh, Dennis…

DENNIS. Yes.

MARGARET. Dennis.

DENNIS. I only…

MARGARET. This is crazy.

DENNIS. I only chatted her up because I knew she knew you. I only went *out* with her because I knew she knew you, because it was you I needed to… (*Beat.*) Do you not understand what I'm saying?

MARGARET. Hang on a second. (*Beat.*) So, you used her.

DENNIS. Who?

MARGARET. Adele.

DENNIS. Oh, well, listen, I…

MARGARET. Dennis…

DENNIS. …I like Adele a *lot*…

MARGARET. But you used her.

DENNIS. I…

MARGARET. …to get to *me*, Dennis, Jesus, my fucking *daughter*, and I should be what…?

DENNIS. You…

MARGARET. …flattered? This is unbelievable.

DENNIS. No.

MARGARET. …Impressed? At your honesty?

DENNIS. At my extremes.

MARGARET. Your extremes.

DENNIS. That I've gone to, Margaret. This isn't me. This…

MARGARET. You know what? You have to get out of this house.

DENNIS. Margaret…

MARGARET. You have to go. Do you know how deceitful what you've done is…?

DENNIS. I know.

MARGARET....how cruel?

DENNIS. I don't mean to be cruel, Margaret.

MARGARET. Well...

DENNIS. *Or* deceitful, I...

MARGARET. Look: you need to leave right now and never come back, Dennis, and never contact my daughter again.

DENNIS. Margaret...

MARGARET. Now! Please! Or I'll call my husband, and I won't be responsible, when I tell him, Christ, what you've told me, for what he'll do.

DENNIS. What will he do? Hurt me?

MARGARET. *Yes*.

DENNIS. Okay, well...

MARGARET. *Yes*, he'll hurt you. You'd better fucking believe it.

DENNIS. All right, look: I'm sorry. I'm in a state. I'm sorry. But, if you could only give me a minute, just to say what I need to, what I *came* to say, then I'll go and I'll never, like you asked, ever come in contact, with *her*, with *you*...

MARGARET. Who's 'her'?

DENNIS....with Adele again. I swear to God. And...

MARGARET. Go.

DENNIS. What?

MARGARET. Go.

DENNIS (*beat*). Leave?

MARGARET. No, speak. Say what you have to say and be quick. *Then* you can leave, I can't even fucking look at you!

Silence.

DENNIS. I think I can heal you.

MARGARET. Heal me?

DENNIS. Yes.

MARGARET. Of what?

DENNIS. Your sadness.

MARGARET. Jesus Christ. (*Beat*.) I can't be healed.

DENNIS. I think you can. In your present circumstances you can't, but I think you can.

MARGARET. My present circumstances.

DENNIS. Yes.

MARGARET. Meaning what?

DENNIS. The man you're with, no offence to him; the house you're in...

MARGARET. Dennis...

DENNIS. No, listen: Let me...

MARGARET. ...Fuck!

DENNIS. I'm saying, see, to break away from it all, all that stuff that's holding you back, to break away and to engage in, to commit to something that'd overwhelm you, that'd...

MARGARET. Overwhelm me.

DENNIS. Yes... that'd obsess and consume you, like a deeply fucking intense, like, love affair, say...

MARGARET. Jesus...

DENNIS. ...a passionate...

MARGARET. ...Christ, I've less fucking interest, Dennis, in passion. (*Beat*.) What the hell?!

DENNIS. Right. (*Beat*) Well, can I say something?

MARGARET. What?

DENNIS. This is gonna sound really arrogant or presumptuous, maybe, but I think you're wrong? And if we were to do it once...

MARGARET. Do what?

DENNIS....to make love once – No, wait – and it doesn't have to be here, or tonight, it could be another time, but I think you'd see. So much of you is lying dormant.

MARGARET. Lying...

DENNIS. Yes, and if it was...

MARGARET. Right.

DENNIS....was to be awakened... Why are you laughing?

MARGARET. No reason.

DENNIS. All right. Well, to hell with sex. It doesn't even have to *be* about sex. There's comfort...

MARGARET. Right.

DENNIS....companionship, you know?... devotion. Look: that guy...

MARGARET. What guy?

DENNIS. Your husband.

MARGARET. Michael.

DENNIS....He isn't good enough. I can see it. He doesn't give enough. I wouldn't allow you to sleep on the sofa bed.

MARGARET. I already said that I *need* to.

DENNIS. Well...

MARGARET. That I *prefer* to. And he *is* good enough, Dennis. How dare you?

DENNIS. So, why are you still unhappy?

MARGARET. Why? Because...

DENNIS. Look: I know it's really hard for you to let go, but...

MARGARET. Let go of what?

DENNIS. Of your son. I understand there's no, you know, closure for you and that he's in your life every day, and you think you can never move on, but you can, or at least you can a little bit. I mean, look at us.

MARGARET. What?

DENNIS. The two of us. Even the symmetry of it. I lost my
  parents, you lost your child. Maybe...

MARGARET. So?

DENNIS. Well, there's a symmetry in it. Or it's a sign, or, you
  know what? Maybe each of us could provide for the other
  something the other lacks. If you came away with me...

MARGARET. Where? To Paris?

DENNIS. Yeah, if you wanted...

MARGARET. Dennis...

DENNIS....why not? And I'd give up, I'll tell you what else,
  I'd give up my studies, my, seriously, my ambitions... If you
  agreed to, I would.

MARGARET....To come with you.

DENNIS. Yes I would, but what I'm saying is, wherever we
  went, or whether we went anywhere at all, I would,
  Margaret, I would promise, I'm promising *now*, to take care
  of you, to devote myself to your healing, your happiness, for
  the rest of my life.

MARGARET. Jesus...

DENNIS. You think I don't mean it?

MARGARET....Dennis...

DENNIS. Do you? Tell me you think I don't mean it.

  Long pause.

MARGARET. I know you do.

DENNIS. I can't help this. I don't know how it happened. Why
  that day? Why you? Why do I feel how I feel to this fucking
  extent? Because my heart feels ready to burst with it,
  Margaret. (*Beat.*) To burst with it.

  Long pause. He is crying now.

I've been so fucking unhappy since that day.

MARGARET. What day?

DENNIS. In Brown Thomas. Why didn't you say hello when I said hello?

MARGARET. Dennis…

DENNIS. Were you ignoring me?

MARGARET. I don't think I even saw you.

DENNIS. I've been so unhappy because I thought I'd never see you again and I never *believed* I would, and now that I do… now that I'm here… Oh, fuck it… And *you're* here… Fuck it. Fuck it…

Silence.

MARGARET. Dennis. (*Pause.*) Dennis.

DENNIS. What?

MARGARET (*pause*). I love my husband, Dennis. You say he doesn't give enough, but the things he's put up with from me, and *for* me, you wouldn't believe; the fact that he's stayed with me when any other man would have run away, is… is testament, to…

DENNIS. Come on.

MARGARET.…to his loyalty, his… 'Come on' what?

DENNIS. And who says *I* wouldn't be?

MARGARET. Loyal?

DENNIS. Yes.

MARGARET. To someone in my situation?

DENNIS. Yes.

MARGARET. But you don't even *know* my situation, Dennis.

DENNIS. Yes, I do.

MARGARET. You don't. You think you do, but you don't. And I can only imagine what you're going through, the intensity…

DENNIS. No, you can't.

MARGARET. I can... of what you're feeling. I can, and I'm sorry. I am. And I sympathise with this... (*Beat.*)

DENNIS....love.

MARGARET....with this love you feel, this want, but I can't be responsible for it. (*Beat.*) I can't. And I can't encourage it, and I certainly can't, and never *will*, Dennis, act upon it. Do you understand me?

DENNIS (*pause*). Yes.

MARGARET....Ever.

Silence.

And now you have to go.

DENNIS. I...

MARGARET. Dennis.

DENNIS. Fuck! (*Pause.*) Fuck!

MARGARET. Dennis.

DENNIS. Why can't you just fucking *do* it?

MARGARET. What?

DENNIS. *Love* me!

MARGARET (*beat*). I...

DENNIS. Why? (*Pause.*) Do you know how easy it'd be? Just *decide* to.

MARGARET. What?

DENNIS. Just *decide* to love me. (*Pause.*) Why can't you *do* that?

MARGARET (*pause*). I...

DENNIS. Why can't you just decide to *love* me?

Black.

Interlude

Fade up on MARGARET, *asleep on a sofa bed. Again, it is before dawn, and again the light is vague, abstract. On the low coffee table beside her sits the glass and a half-full bottle of whiskey.* MICHAEL, *semi-dressed, enters from upstairs, takes the whiskey bottle and glass to the kitchen area, puts the bottle back in the press, rinses the glass at the sink, then goes to the sofa bed and sits down on its edge, touching* MARGARET's *shoulder. She wakes, sits up. They embrace, again exchanging several words which we don't hear.* MARGARET *gets off the sofa bed, puts on her dressing gown, and exits upstairs.* MICHAEL *folds the duvet, places it on an armchair. He removes the sheet from the bed, puts it on top of the duvet, takes the pillow, puts it on top of the sheet. He folds the bed away, remaking the sofa, replacing the last couple of cushions. He picks up the duvet cover, sheet and pillow. Pause. He sits down on the sofa, stares dully at the floor. Silence.*

Fade to black.

ACT TWO

Scene One

The room is empty. It is afternoon. We hear the front door open and close.

ADELE (*calling; offstage*). It's just me!

    Pause. ADELE *enters.*

Mam? (*Pause.*) Dad?

    She goes back out to the stairs, calls up them:

Mam?

    She re-enters, taking out her phone, dials. Pause. Then, into it:

Hey. Where are you? (*Beat.*) Ah, right! (*Beat.*) I'm here in the house… Yeah. No, I just dropped over and… (*Beat.*) No, sure it's my own fault for not having called you first. And, so… (*Beat.*) Uh-huh. (*Beat.*) Uh-huh. No, that's fine. No, he's not here either, unless… (*Beat.*) No, he might be, actually. I'll have a check in a minute. (*Pause.*) No, I know. All right, well, look: I'll see… (*Beat.*) I am, yeah… No, sure it was just for a chat, that's all, sure I'm fine. (*Beat.*) Yeah. (*Pause.*) No, I bet you he *is* in the shed. All right. Talk later, Mam. Talk later. Bye.

    She hangs up, goes to the stage-left window, looks out. Silence. The doorbell rings. She exits to the hall, taking off her coat. We hear the front door open, then a male voice:

VOICE (*offstage*). Hey.

ADELE (*offstage*). Hello.

VOICE (*offstage*). How are things?

ADELE (*offstage*). All right, yeah.

VOICE (*pause; offstage*). I wonder if I could talk to you.

ADELE (*offstage*). Talk to me?

VOICE (*offstage*). Yeah.

ADELE (*offstage*). Well…

VOICE (*offstage*). Just for a couple of minutes?

ADELE (*long pause; offstage*). All right. Come in.

VOICE (*offstage*). Cheers.

> *We hear the front door close.* GARY *and* ADELE, *now without her coat, enter.*

GARY. Not as bad as it was out there, now.

ADELE. Huh? Oh…

GARY. The weather.

ADELE.…right. No, it isn't, actually.

GARY. How are your folks?

ADELE. Okay.

GARY. Are they here?

ADELE. My dad's in the shed, I think.

GARY. You 'think'?

ADELE. I just arrived myself.

GARY. Ah, right. (*Beat.*) Probably lucky I caught you, then, I suppose. The plan was actually…

ADELE. What?

GARY.…was to get your number and call you. *Off* your parents…

ADELE. Right.

GARY.…and call you.

ADELE. Why?

GARY. Well, I wanted to ask you if you might want to go for a drink or something at some point.

ADELE (*beat*). A drink in a pub.

GARY. Yeah.

ADELE. Why?

GARY. Or a coffee, maybe. Well, to talk about Belinda.

ADELE. Right. You know what? I wouldn't really be into doing that, Gary.

GARY. Oh. (*Beat.*) Why not?

ADELE. I just wouldn't.

GARY. Okay.

ADELE. But, if you wanna say what you wanna say right *now…*

GARY. Okay. Well, is that okay?

ADELE. That's fine.

GARY. All right, well… (*Beat.*) do you mind if I sit?

ADELE. Go ahead.

GARY. All right.

He goes to the table and sits. Beat. Then, standing up again:

Do you mind if I take off my coat, actually?

She shakes her head.

Cool.

He takes off his coat, hangs it on the back of his chair, sits back down again. ADELE *remains standing in the living-room area.*

So, what did you think of the funeral?

ADELE. What did I think of it?

GARY. How did you think it went?

ADELE. I dunno.

GARY. I thought it was pretty good, to be honest.

ADELE. What do you mean?

GARY. Like, well-attended.

ADELE. Right.

GARY. I actually never realised she'd that many friends.

ADELE. Well, she was pretty well-liked.

GARY. Mm. (*Beat*.) No, I know. (*Long pause*.) Lot of sadness there.

ADELE. In the church?

GARY. *And* later on. At the…

ADELE. Mm.

GARY.…the burial…

ADELE. Right.

GARY.…the afters, whatever.

ADELE (*beat*). There was all right.

GARY (*long pause*). I have to say, I've been finding it pretty hard to cope these last few days. As I'm sure *you* have.

ADELE. Uh-huh.

GARY. Been feeling pretty bewildered, to be honest. Cos I just… I never saw it…

ADELE. Right.

GARY.…I mean, at all. Saw it coming, like. And I wanted to ask you, I suppose, if she ever gave *you* any indication.

ADELE. Of what?

GARY. Well, as to why she did it.

ADELE. Right.

GARY. I mean, was she depressed? Or…

ADELE. Was she *depressed*?!

GARY.…Or upset about something? Yeah, cos I never saw it.

ADELE. No?

GARY. I never saw *any*thing. Seriously, I'm in the dark, Adele.
I mean, I know you and I have our differences, or, you know,
have had in the past, but I thought, if we could put that aside
in our, I dunno, our mutual grieving...

ADELE. Our what?

GARY. ...you know, our mourning of her. (*Beat.*) Cos we loved
her, didn't we?

ADELE. Yeah...

GARY. In our different ways.

ADELE. ...well, I know *I* did.

GARY. Mm. (*Pause.*) What do you mean?

ADELE. What?

GARY. You say that like you're saying I didn't.

ADELE. Well, you didn't.

GARY. What are you talking about?

ADELE. You didn't love her.

GARY. Why would...

ADELE. You couldn't have.

GARY. Why would you go and say something like that? (*Beat.*)
You don't know how I feel.

ADELE. I know how you treated her.

GARY. How?

ADELE (*beat*). You abused her, Gary.

GARY. What?!

ADELE. Come on...

GARY. I abused her?!

ADELE. ...the whole time, yes, the whole time you were
together, you treated her like...

GARY. No, I didn't.

ADELE. ...like shit. You fucking did.

GARY. How the hell would you know, anyway?

ADELE. How would I know?

GARY. Yeah.

ADELE. I was her best friend, Gary. God, do you think she…

GARY. Look…

ADELE. Hang on. Do you think she never told me things?

GARY. Like what?

ADELE. Like everything.

GARY. 'Everything'! What did she tell you?

ADELE. She told me how you demeaned her…

GARY. Demeaned her?

ADELE. Yes.

GARY. I…

ADELE. …every chance you got. She told me about your *lies*, about your constant…

GARY. My…

ADELE. …your manipu*l*ations… I heard it *all* from her, Gary.

GARY. Adele…

ADELE. I heard about the *things* you made her do.

GARY. What things?

ADELE (*beat*). You know what I'm talking about.

GARY. Listen to me…

ADELE. She fucking despised them.

GARY. …Listen: (*Pause.*) I'm pretty pissed off, for one, she'd divulge such…

ADELE. Well, she did.

GARY. …such intimate stuff, such private stuff, and for two, she didn't despise them, she liked them.

ADELE. She pretended to like, and she didn't *even*, Gary, she endured them, that's all, she allowed them and knew better than to refuse, and knew better than to complain, for fear...

GARY. Knew better?

ADELE. Yes.

GARY. For fear of what?

ADELE. ...of you leaving her if she did, cos she knew she only ever had you by the skin of her... didn't she?

GARY. Didn't she what?

ADELE. Only ever have you by the skin of her teeth!

GARY. No.

ADELE. That's a lie.

GARY. She didn't. We wouldn't have been together so long if she did...

ADELE. Gary...

GARY. ...would we? No, fuck *you*, Adele, you know nothing about our relationship except what Belinda told you.

ADELE. Exactly.

GARY. Nothing about how *I* felt for *her*, nothing about how I feel now she's fucking... (*Beat*.) now that she's gone.

ADELE. Oh, stop, would you?

GARY. How can you look at me and...

ADELE. What.

GARY. ...and see my devastation and still...

ADELE. Your devastation?!

GARY. Yes.

ADELE. Are you kidding me?! You're mildly fucking put out at most. You never cared for her. All she was was your fucking... I don't know what.

GARY. What was she?

ADELE. *I* don't know. Your lapdog...

GARY. Adele…

ADELE.…Your victim. The things you did, I swear, how can you have had anything but contempt for her?

GARY. The things we did… (*Beat*.) *Adele*: the things we did were consensual…

ADELE. No.

GARY.…and if they weren't, then she should've…

ADELE. She couldn't.

GARY.…she should've said. Well, that's *her* fucking problem, Adele.

ADELE. It was.

GARY. What?

ADELE. It *was* her fucking problem, Gary. She's dead.

GARY. I know she is.

   Long pause.

   Let me tell you something. Can I…

ADELE. Yes.

GARY.…Can I tell you something?

ADELE. Go on.

GARY. All right. Sit down, will you?

ADELE. What?

GARY. Sit down for a minute.

ADELE. I *won't* sit down for a minute, *no*.

GARY (*beat*). All right. (*Pause.*) All right. (*Pause.*) So I did, sometimes, like, fair enough, not treat her well. I'll admit it.

ADELE. Right.

GARY. I'm admitting it, right? But can I tell you the truest thing, Adele? And this is from the bottom of my heart, all right? (*Pause.*) Okay?

ADELE. Mm-hm.

GARY. Sometimes a person loves another person so much and needs that love returned, so much, that they, yes, they mistreat that person. You know why?

ADELE. Why?

GARY. And this is me, I'm saying. Well, because, deep inside, they don't believe they're worthy. And so...

ADELE. What?!

GARY....they...

ADELE. Gary!

GARY....I'm telling you, and so they continually, they test the other person. They push and they, absolutely, treat that person badly, and then they say, 'Well, if she can put, you know...'

ADELE. Christ.

GARY. '...put up with that, then maybe she does.'

ADELE. What?

GARY. Love me. Maybe she actually does, you know? I mean, and I know it's a terrible way to treat a person. I do, but it comes from the, seriously, the deepest fucking insecurity, the deepest *terror*, Adele, of not being loved... of not being loved, of not, like I said, being *worthy* of love. I don't know, because...

ADELE. Gary.

GARY. What?

ADELE. Just stop, all right?

GARY. Adele...

ADELE. You know something? There's always a straw.

GARY. A straw.

ADELE. A final straw. And to hell with your 'insecurity', Jesus, if you had've cut her fucking arm off, she *still* would've went to the ends of the earth for you. If you had've plucked her eyes out... I mean, she loved you to an...

GARY. And I loved her, Adele!

ADELE (*on 'Adele'*)....to an unbelievable fucking degree, and she proved it a thousand times fucking over with what she suffered from you...

GARY. Adele...

ADELE. Hang on, now... with what she endured. But the thing you have to realise, Gary, is that the reward for that endurance, the one thing that made her capable of it, was the fact that you were *hers*...

GARY. Uh-huh.

ADELE....do you understand?... was...

GARY. No.

ADELE....was the fact that you belonged to her, Gary. To *her*. And as long as you did... (*Beat*.) She killed... (*Pause*.) You know why she killed herself?

GARY. Why?

ADELE. Because she knew she'd lost you.

GARY. What?!

ADELE. That's why.

GARY. Because she knew she'd *lost* me?!

ADELE. Yes.

GARY. But she hadn't lost me, Adele. What the hell are you...?

ADELE. Who was the other girl?

GARY. What other...? (*Beat*.) Fucking Donna?

ADELE. Was that her name?

GARY. Ah, Jesus. That was just a suggestion!

ADELE. Well, that suggestion did it, Gary. 'Share you with her...'?!

GARY. Yeah.

ADELE....are you fucking mad?! Did you love her?

GARY. Donna?

ADELE. Yes.

GARY. No, I didn't. I don't give a fuck about Donna.

ADELE. Well, Belinda said otherwise, Gary.

GARY. What?

ADELE. Belinda told me that you said you were in love with her.

GARY. That I said…

ADELE. Yes.

GARY. Well that's bullshit, Adele. I mean, I told her maybe I cared for the girl…

ADELE. Oh, come on!

GARY. …but love her? No.

ADELE. So…

GARY. …the way I did Belinda? Absolutely not.

ADELE. So, why did you want them…

GARY. I told you.

ADELE. …want them to share you?

GARY. I told you, it was a test. I needed to…

ADELE. Right.

GARY. …to confirm…

ADELE. … her love for you.

GARY. Yes! Do you get me now?

ADELE. To test it.

GARY. Yes! You know what this is? It's so fucked up, I know.

ADELE. It is.

GARY. But, you know what this is, Adele? A purging.

ADELE. A what?

GARY. To admit all this. To confess. It's a purging, and this may sound completely fucking mad, but I'm grateful…

ADELE. You…

GARY. …for the opportunity. Yes. To you for giving me it, because…

ADELE. Gary.

GARY. What?

ADELE. Can I ask you a really serious question?

GARY. Of course you can.

ADELE. Do you have some kind of fucking… autism or something?

GARY (*beat*). What are you talking about?

ADELE. Something that prevents yourself from seeing beyond yourself. Like when someone's in pain…

GARY. Uh-huh.

ADELE. …can you see that they're in pain?

GARY. Of course I can.

ADELE. But does it mean anything to you?

GARY. Yes.

ADELE. So, how can you be so cruel, so self-fucking-centred, as to…

GARY. Fuck you, I told you.

ADELE. What did you tell me?

GARY. Forget it. I'm not gonna tell you again.

ADELE. You killed her, Gary. You made her life a fucking misery and… a *daily* fucking misery, and then you killed her. You're fucking… and you know you did. You're a scumbag…

GARY. Fuck you.

ADELE. …you're a disgrace, and, you know what?

GARY. And you're a fucking bitch, Adele.

ADELE. You know what? And maybe I am, but, you know what? If you were in any way capable of shame, and which I can see you're not, you'd be hanging your fucking head right now. You wouldn't be hanging your head, you wouldn't *be* here, cos you wouldn't be able to show your fucking face. (*Beat.*) Now, could you go, please? I really don't wanna talk to you any more.

GARY (*long pause*). Fair enough.

He gets up and puts on his jacket. Then, after several moments:

I loved her.

ADELE. So you keep insisting.

GARY. I did. And what she did is gonna haunt me the rest of my fucking…

ADELE. Good.

GARY.…my life. And you're the one who's autistic, Adele, if you can't show any sympathy for, or, you know, any understanding of…

ADELE. Right.

GARY.…of other people's pain. You're the one who's fucked up.

As he goes:

ADELE. How's the car, by the way?

He stops, turns back to her.

GARY. The car?

ADELE. Yeah.

GARY. Why?

ADELE. No, just, it must be great not to have to pay back the fifteen grand you borrowed off her to pay for it.

GARY. I…

ADELE. Although you were never going to anyway, were you?

GARY. You know what, Adele?

ADELE. What?

GARY. I could never fucking abide you.

ADELE. Could you not? Well, the feeling's mutual, Gary.

GARY. You know why?

ADELE. Why?

GARY. Becau…

We hear the back door open, then close. Beat.

ADELE. Dad?

MICHAEL (*offstage*). Adele!

MICHAEL enters, his hands covered in oil.

…Hey! What are *you* doing here?!

ADELE. You remember Gary.

MICHAEL. Oh, yeah. Sure we met at the funeral. (*Heading for the sink.*) How are things?

GARY. All right.

MICHAEL (*washing his hands*). So, to what do we owe the honour, Adele?

ADELE. Just thought I'd drop up.

MICHAEL. Right. (*Beat.*) Your mother's in Marie's, I think.

ADELE. She is. I just spoke to her.

Silence.

GARY. All right. (*Going.*) I'm gone.

MICHAEL. Bye, Gary.

ADELE. Think about what I said, Gary, won't you?

He stops, turns, stares at her. Pause.

GARY. You're a fucking cunt, Adele, you know that?

He turns, exits to the hall.

MICHAEL. What the f…?

He goes after him, leaving the tap running.

Hang on a second, there. (*Beat*.) Hang on a second, she's what?

ADELE. Dad.

MICHAEL. You called her a what?

He catches up to him in the hall. They are both now offstage:

ADELE. Dad.

GARY (*offstage*). Nothing.

ADELE follows them, stopping in the doorway.

MICHAEL (*offstage*). Say what you fucking said.

GARY (*offstage*). I said, she's a bitter, nasty-minded little *cuooomph!* What the fuck?!

ADELE. Dad!

GARY (*offstage*). *Oomph! Agh!* You fucking...

ADELE. Dad!

We hear the sounds of a scuffle. Then:

GARY (*offstage*). *Oomph! Oomph!*

ADELE. Dad, stop!

MICHAEL (*offstage*). Get out.

We hear the front door open.

Talk about *my* fucking daughter that way, you fucking...

ADELE. Dad!

MICHAEL.... you little prick, you! Out!

GARY (*offstage*). Fuck you.

MICHAEL (*offstage*). Go on!

GARY. (*offstage; beat; then, as if from the street*). Fuck you, you...

He is cut off by the sound of the door slamming shut. Silence.
MICHAEL enters, passing ADELE.

ADELE. What are you doing?

He returns to the sink, resumes washing his hands.

Dad.

MICHAEL. Adele.

ADELE. What?

MICHAEL. Leave it. Seriously.

ADELE. Why did you have to hit him?

MICHAEL. Because he deserved it.

ADELE. No, he didn't deserve it. What are you talking about?

MICHAEL. He was rude. I'm sorry.

ADELE. Rude?!

MICHAEL. Insulting. I'm not gonna let him talk like that. To *you*?

ADELE. But…

MICHAEL. Or *about* you? No. No.

ADELE. So *don't* let him talk like that, but to, fucking hell, to act like a savage…

MICHAEL. Adele…

ADELE. What?

MICHAEL. …don't. I did what I had to.

ADELE. Why did you have to? Was he not going anyway?

MICHAEL. Yes.

ADELE. So why did you have to?

MICHAEL. Because he insulted you.

ADELE. So?

MICHAEL. In my house.

ADELE. And that merits a beating?

MICHAEL. It was a couple of slaps, Adele.

ADELE. You call that a couple of slaps?

MICHAEL *turns off the tap*.

Dad.

He dries his hands.

It sickens me, you know that? When I see you behave that way. It actually makes me feel, I'm sorry to say it, disgust at you...

MICHAEL. Disgust?

ADELE. ...at that part of you, yes, and worse, it frightens me to death. It always has.

MICHAEL. What do you mean it always has? When have I ever...? When have you ever seen me be violent?

ADELE. I've seen it.

MICHAEL. When?

ADELE. Jesus, several times. I saw it with that guy who went out with Kathleen...

MICHAEL. That guy...

ADELE. ...I saw it...

MICHAEL. ...That guy was a bully, Adele. He...

ADELE. I saw it in Rathmines. And I don't care what he was.

MICHAEL. In Rathmines?

ADELE. In that couple's house we used to go to. George...

MICHAEL. Right.

ADELE. ...George and Anne.

MICHAEL. Twenty-five fucking years ago?

ADELE. Exactly. And I still remember.

MICHAEL. Do you know what he did?

ADELE. I don't care what he did.

MICHAEL. He dragged your brother through his house by the hair.

ADELE. Jonathan?

MICHAEL. Seven years old.

ADELE. Why?

MICHAEL. It doesn't matter why. For flooding his bathroom.

ADELE. On purpose?

MICHAEL. Of course on purpose. I still wasn't gonna let the fucker away with it.

ADELE. Dad...

MICHAEL. The same with Gary.

ADELE. ...It isn't justification enough.

MICHAEL. To give them a hiding?

ADELE. I hate that phrase. But, yes.

MICHAEL. Right.

ADELE. Yes. It isn't. Nothing is.

MICHAEL. Well, that's where we differ.

ADELE. And those weren't the only times...

MICHAEL. I have never...

ADELE. ...were they?

MICHAEL. Adele... I have never put my hand on anybody who wasn't threatening... When you're a, listen: when you're a parent yourself, love, come back and try and tell me you wouldn't do anything to, *anything*... to protect your family or your family's dignity...

ADELE. Or *what*?!

MICHAEL. ...or maybe, you know, it's a gender thing...

ADELE. Their 'dignity'?!

MICHAEL. Their honour.

ADELE. Jesus, a 'gender thing'?!

MICHAEL. A male thing.

ADELE. Right.

MICHAEL. The instinct to protect, with a man, is just… it's powerful, love, and…

ADELE. I don't think it's *about* protection, Dad.

MICHAEL. What do you think it's about?

ADELE. It's about temper.

MICHAEL. Temper?

ADELE. It's about, yes. It's about lack of control, it's about having a nature that's aggressive, that's violent, and that, I think, you think there's something cool about…

MICHAEL. Cool.

ADELE.…or romantic, yeah, about being that way, but there isn't.

MICHAEL. I don't.

ADELE. Well, I think you do, Dad.

MICHAEL. Well, there isn't really much I can *do* about that!

ADELE. I think you do.

MICHAEL. *Okay! Fuck me!*

ADELE. What happened with Dennis?

MICHAEL (*beat*). Dennis?!

ADELE. Yeah.

MICHAEL. What are you talking about?

ADELE. Why haven't I seen him?

MICHAEL. I…

ADELE. Or heard from him.

MICHAEL. *Have* you not heard from him?

ADELE. No.

MICHAEL. Since when?

ADELE. Since the night he visited, Dad. Why won't he return my calls?

MICHAEL. How the hell should I know?

ADELE. What did you do to him?

MICHAEL. Nothing. He…

ADELE. Or say to him.

MICHAEL. Nothing.

ADELE. He left.

MICHAEL. That's right.

ADELE. When?

MICHAEL. Before we got up. I already told you that. We both did.

ADELE. Yeah, so, why amen't I able to contact him?

MICHAEL. I don't know.

ADELE. What was said? Surely something was said that night that…

MICHAEL. No.

ADELE.…or argued about…

MICHAEL. Like what?

ADELE. I don't know. The weather.

MICHAEL. Nothing was argued about, and I wonder if he wasn't just a fella who decided, I don't know, who…

ADELE. What?

MICHAEL. I don't like the way you're accusing me, Adele!

ADELE. Who decided what?

MICHAEL.…that a girl who put some other relationship over one she had with him maybe wasn't worth it.

ADELE. What other relationship? Belinda?

MICHAEL. Yes.

ADELE. But I explained that to him.

MICHAEL. So?

ADELE. He understood.

MICHAEL. He said he did.

ADELE. What do you mean?

MICHAEL. Nothing, I just…

ADELE. Did he say something?

MICHAEL. No, I'm just off… you know, offering a theory.

ADELE. Right.

MICHAEL. There could be a load of them.

ADELE. Such as?

MICHAEL. I don't know. He might be a prick, *despite* how he came across; he mightn't have felt for you as much as you thought he did; he might be a coward who prefers, when he's dumping a girl, to avoid her and hope she'll get the message, rather than…

ADELE. How dare you?

MICHAEL.…rather than… Listen: you're the one who asked, and it's only a theory in any case. I could give you a hundred.

ADELE. He did.

MICHAEL. What?

ADELE. Love me!

MICHAEL. I'm not saying he didn't, I… (*Pause.*) What do *you* think happened?

ADELE. I think you're responsible, Dad. I think you got into an argument and you probably did something.

MICHAEL. Did something.

ADELE. Yes.

MICHAEL. Like what?

ADELE. Like hurt him. Like told him, I don't know, to stay away from me or you'd hurt him *again*.

MICHAEL. But, why?

ADELE. I don't know.

MICHAEL. Why would I? Look, you know what? Adele, you know what? I don't want to patronise you, but this is a very emotional time for you anyway...

ADELE. You *are* patronising me.

MICHAEL....what with Belinda and all, and I think...

ADELE. You *are* patronising me, Dad.

MICHAEL. Well, I'm sorry, but I'm not gonna entertain any more the suggestions you're making. (*Beat.*) To hell with that.

ADELE. You're not.

MICHAEL. To hell with it. No, I'm not.

ADELE. Where is he, Dad?

MICHAEL. Adele...

ADELE. Where is he? What did you do to him?

MICHAEL. Jesus...

ADELE. What did you do to him? What did you do to Jonathan?

MICHAEL (*beat*). *Jonathan?!*

ADELE. What did you do to my brother?

MICHAEL (*pause*). Adele...

ADELE. Tell me!

MICHAEL....darling...

ADELE. Tell me what you did to my brother!

Black.

Scene Two

MARGARET *sits alone at the kitchen table, drinking tea. It is evening of the following day. A knock on the front door. She goes out to the hall. We hear the door open. Beat.*

MARGARET (*offstage*). Why are you knocking?

ADELE (*offstage*). What?

MARGARET (*offstage*). Why didn't you just come in?

We hear the front door close.

ADELE (*offstage*). I dunno. It kinda didn't seem right, given, you know...

MARGARET (*offstage*). Right.

ADELE (*offstage*)....me and Dad.

MARGARET (*offstage*). Come in. Come in.

As they enter:

ADELE. Is he here?

MARGARET. I told you he wouldn't be. And that's stupid.

ADELE. What is?

MARGARET. Not to use your key. As if you had to get permission to enter or something.

ADELE. Well...

MARGARET. He's gone into town. It's Richard Farrell's birthday.

ADELE. Who?

MARGARET. A fellow he knows in work. Do you want a cup of tea?

ADELE. All right.

MARGARET. There's a few of them gone in for a meal to celebrate.

She goes to get the tea while ADELE sits down. Pause.

So, how are you?

ADELE. How am I?

MARGARET. Yeah.

ADELE. I'm a mess.

MARGARET. Sure how else would you be, I suppose.

ADELE. I keep… Exactly.

MARGARET.… You know?

ADELE. I dunno, I find I keep getting upset at the most inconvenient moments.

MARGARET. Really?

ADELE. Yeah.

MARGARET. Like when?

ADELE. At the gym…

MARGARET. No.

ADELE. Yeah, on the treadmill, twice, I've burst into tears.

MARGARET. Oh, Adele.

ADELE. I know.

MARGARET (*bringing the tea*). Of course, it's those times, when your mind is free to wander, isn't it…

ADELE. What.

MARGARET.… that you get upset.

ADELE. I suppose. Everyone looking at me, 'What the hell's going on with her?'

MARGARET. Don't mind them.

ADELE. I don't.

MARGARET *sits*. *Pause*.

Fucking waste.

MARGARET. Huh?

ADELE. Belinda.

MARGARET. Oh.

ADELE. Fucking asshole.

MARGARET. Gary?

ADELE. You should have seen him, Mam. Sitting there, completely free of any, whatever… responsibility…

MARGARET. Right.

ADELE. …or guilt. 'What was it, Adele…?'

MARGARET. This is him.

ADELE. … 'What the,' yeah, 'What the hell could have made her do what she did?'

MARGARET. As if he didn't know.

ADELE. Well, exactly.

MARGARET. Right.

ADELE. You know what he said? You know what reason he gave in the end for why he treated her like…? Ah, to hell with it.

MARGARET. What?

ADELE. No, to hell with it, Mam. It's not even worth repeating.

MARGARET. All right.

ADELE. He's poison.

MARGARET. Uh-huh.

ADELE. He is. He's *worse* than scum, and yet he's the one still swanning around, you know? while she's in a, fuck, a box…

MARGARET. Mm-hm.

ADELE. …in the ground. So fucking unfair!

MARGARET. I know.

ADELE. So unjust! What the hell *is* it with men?

MARGARET. I know. Well…

ADELE. Seriously.

MARGARET. Well, not all men are like that, Adele.

ADELE. Enough of them are.

MARGARET. Right.

ADELE. Fucking Dennis…?

MARGARET. Have you heard from him yet?

ADELE (*pause*). I went to see him yesterday.

MARGARET. No.

ADELE. Another asshole. Yeah, I called to the pub he works in and threatened to make a scene if he didn't talk to me.

MARGARET. Okay.

ADELE. So…

MARGARET. Wow.

ADELE. I know. I actually couldn't believe it myself.

MARGARET. And what did he say?

ADELE. Well, we're not *together* any more.

MARGARET. Oh, no…!

ADELE. *That's* finished.

MARGARET.…Adele!

ADELE. It's all right. It's fine.

MARGARET. And what did he say about never getting in touch?

ADELE (*pause*). He said he'd needed to spend some time alone…

MARGARET. Okay.

ADELE.…because… agh…!

MARGARET. What?

ADELE.…nothing. He had some bullshit excuse involving you.

MARGARET. Me?

ADELE. You and Dad. You don't even wanna hear it.

MARGARET. I do.

ADELE. Some nonsense about how, I dunno, having met you, and having seen the level of love you had for me and how invested you were in my… (*Beat.*)

MARGARET. Your future?

ADELE. …my happiness.

MARGARET. Right.

ADELE. *And* my future, yeah, he realised he needed to have an honest think about whether or not he actually wanted to take that step, to…

MARGARET. Which?

ADELE. …or to make that commitment. Just in deciding whether me and him were gonna be long-term.

MARGARET. Right.

ADELE. And after a bit of, how did he put it?… self-examination, he decided he didn't…

MARGARET. Self-examination.

ADELE. Yeah… that he wasn't ready yet.

MARGARET. What an eejit!

ADELE. Mm.

MARGARET (*pause*). It's his loss, Adele.

ADELE. You know what really annoys me, though?

MARGARET. What.

ADELE. He was the one who was pushing it.

MARGARET. Pushing…

ADELE. Us, like. Wanting to meet you and Dad or whatever.

MARGARET. Really?!

ADELE. Yes.

MARGARET. It was him who…

ADELE. That's what I'm saying. I mean, he was moving a bit too fast for me in any case. But, to be honest… I dunno…

MARGARET. What?

ADELE (*beat*)….it was kind of wonderful too?

MARGARET. Oh, I *know*.

ADELE. So…

MARGARET. I *know*. Oh, Adele, I'm so *sorry*.

ADELE. Don't be. Look: I mean…

MARGARET. Don't be?

ADELE. No. I mean, look: regardless of all that stuff, a man who wouldn't even… I mean, he knew Belinda'd died. He got my messages…

MARGARET. Right.

ADELE.…so he knew how much I needed him. And a man who wouldn't respond to that, even *if* he'd changed his mind about being with me, who wouldn't even send a text so I'd know he was still alive, is, you know what…?

MARGARET. What.

ADELE.…is someone I've really no interest in being with. So I'm glad I found out…

MARGARET. Okay.

ADELE.…when I did, the kind of man he is, you know?

MARGARET. I do.

ADELE. I'm glad.

MARGARET. And what about your father?

ADELE (*beat*). What about him?

MARGARET. Well, I assume you don't believe any more that *he* had anything to…

ADELE. No.

MARGARET....to do with it?

ADELE. Well, could you blame me that I did, though?

MARGARET. Ah, Adele...

ADELE. What.

MARGARET. But, you saw how well they got on.

ADELE. I know I did, but something easily might have been said...

MARGARET....might have been said.

ADELE....or a disagreement might have been had?

MARGARET. About what? And you think that'd cause your father to...

ADELE. Well...

MARGARET....to, what?

ADELE. To threaten him?

MARGARET. Right.

ADELE. To hit him? Well, I mean, given his temperament, Mam.

MARGARET. His...

ADELE. You saw what happened with Gary.

MARGARET. No.

ADELE. Well, you heard.

MARGARET. I *did* hear, yes, and it's bad, it was bad, you're right, and your father *has* had a tendency, on occasion...

ADELE. On occasion?!

MARGARET....to lose the cool. *Yes*, on occasion. To...

ADELE. Right.

MARGARET....to get physical or whatever. But, Jesus, Adele, these things you said. I mean, Jonathan...

ADELE. Mm.

MARGARET....What about what you said about Jonathan? (*Pause*.) I mean, what exactly were you accusing him of?

Long pause.

ADELE. Mam...

MARGARET. What?

ADELE....you know what? Let's not even get into that.

MARGARET. No, let's. (*Pause*.) Let's, Adele. It needs to be gotten into, because what your father told me scared me, love. It really scared me. (*Beat*.) How long have you thought this?

ADELE. What?

MARGARET. Whatever it is you think.

ADELE. I don't.

MARGARET. You don't.

ADELE. It's just something I said in the moment. It's stupid.

MARGARET. Well, if it's stupid, then tell me.

ADELE. No.

MARGARET. Why not?

ADELE. I don't want to. (*Pause*.) Because it *isn't* stupid. Because, if I do, then everything's gonna change.

MARGARET. It's not. Between us?

ADELE. Uh-huh.

MARGARET. But it's not. (*Beat*.) Adele. I promise, whatever you say, I promise, nothing between us will change.

ADELE. You don't know that.

MARGARET. I'm your mother.

ADELE. But you were Jonathan's mother too.

MARGARET. What are you talking about?

ADELE. I heard you.

MARGARET. Who?

ADELE. The night he ran away. All of you.

MARGARET. What did you hear?

ADELE. You crying…

MARGARET. Right.

ADELE.…Dad shouting. I could hear it from my bed, Mam. Calling him vile…

MARGARET. He…

ADELE.…calling him, hang on a second, calling him vile and malignant; calling him, whatever…

MARGARET. Adele…

ADELE.…a fucking animal. What?

MARGARET. You heard that?!

ADELE. Yes.

MARGARET. Why didn't you ever say?

ADELE. Did it happen?

MARGARET. Yes, but…

ADELE. Jesus. (*Beat.*) I think I thought I might have imagined it, or…

MARGARET. Okay.

ADELE.…or invented it? I don't know. He was screaming, Mam…

MARGARET. Who was?

ADELE. Jonathan. Begging Dad not to hurt him…

MARGARET. Adele…

ADELE.…begging Dad not to, begging him to stop, and… What was he doing to him?

MARGARET. Nothing. *You* remember how he used to, don't you?… when we gave out to him…

ADELE. Used to what?

MARGARET. Pretend he was being hurt.

ADELE. I…

MARGARET. Screaming all over the house and accusing us of…

ADELE. No, Mam…

MARGARET.…of abusing… *No?*

ADELE. Or yes…

MARGARET. So…

ADELE.…but this was different. He was scared…

MARGARET. Adele…

ADELE.…he…

MARGARET.…Adele. He was acting.

ADELE. He was in pain.

MARGARET. He was putting it on. Your father never laid a hand on him, love.

ADELE. No.

MARGARET. He…

ADELE. No. Something happened.

MARGARET. Like what?

   Long pause.

   Like what? Oh, Adele…

ADELE. Well, how can he have just disappeared?!

MARGARET. People do. Oh, love…

ADELE.…And never returned!

MARGARET. Kids do.

ADELE. They do, and they're usually dead.

MARGARET. Do *you* think he's dead?

   Silence.

   That's okay.

ADELE. Oh, Mam!

MARGARET. That's okay.

ADELE. I'm sorry.

MARGARET. What are you sorry about?

ADELE. For saying it.

MARGARET. It's okay to say it. It's okay to *think* it. I often think it myself.

ADELE. Do you?

MARGARET. Yes. But, your father...

ADELE. I know.

MARGARET. ...your father certainly didn't...

ADELE. I know. I know. So fucking stupid, I...

MARGARET. Hey.

ADELE. ...I just thought...

MARGARET. What did you think?

ADELE. ...an accident...

MARGARET. Uh-huh.

ADELE. ...a mistake. Like, he hit him and...

MARGARET. Right.

ADELE. ...hit him too hard and... You've always been so fucking evasive about that night...

MARGARET. I...

ADELE. ...you and Dad. So vague.

MARGARET. He ran away, Adele. He...

ADELE (*beat*). I know.

MARGARET. ...and we never saw him again.

ADELE (*pause*). I know.

MARGARET. My poor darling.

Silence.

ADELE. What was it, though?

MARGARET. What do you mean?

ADELE. Why were you crying? Why...

MARGARET. I...

ADELE. Why was he saying those things?

MARGARET. Your father.

ADELE. Calling him, yes...

MARGARET. Well...

ADELE. ...Calling him all those names. What could he have done to make him so angry?

MARGARET. Adele...

ADELE. And why were you so upset?

MARGARET. You've no idea how difficult he was, Adele...

ADELE. Of course I do.

MARGARET. ...how disturbed. But you don't. I know there were things, like that time with the...

ADELE. Mm.

MARGARET. ...the...

ADELE. Go on. The mattress.

MARGARET. Yes.

ADELE. No, I know.

MARGARET. ...but you don't. Not really, Adele. You were only ten, and we...

ADELE. I was nine.

MARGARET. Well...

ADELE. I wasn't *even* ten.

MARGARET. Well, exactly. And we prote... for the most part, we protected you from it.

ADELE. Did you?

MARGARET. Yes.

ADELE. You didn't.

MARGARET. Oh, we did, darling. (*Beat.*) We did.

ADELE. So, what did he do, then?

MARGARET (*beat*). What *things* did he do?

ADELE. No, what did he do that night?

MARGARET (*pause*). I don't really think you need to know.

ADELE. Why not?

MARGARET. Because it won't make things any clearer for you, Adele. Let's just say something bad…

ADELE. Ah, Mam.

MARGARET.…and leave it at that.

ADELE. Let's not.

MARGARET. You know what…?

ADELE. Let's not.

MARGARET. But it's like you were saying earlier, love: if I say it, things will change between us.

ADELE. You and me.

MARGARET. Yes.

ADELE. I don't care. And they won't. I promise.

MARGARET. You don't care.

ADELE. I promise they won't.

MARGARET. Jesus… (*Beat.*) All right. (*Long pause.*) All right. He attacked me.

ADELE. He attacked you.

MARGARET. Yes.

ADELE. In what way?

MARGARET. In a way that he shouldn't have.

ADELE (*beat*). What do you mean?

MARGARET. You know what I mean.

ADELE. I don't.

MARGARET. Adele…

ADELE. Did he hit you?

MARGARET. No.

ADELE. Well, what do you mean, I know what you mean, then?

MARGARET (*beat*). It was sexual.

ADELE. Sexual?!

MARGARET. Yes.

ADELE (*beat*). But he was a child.

MARGARET. I know.

ADELE. So how was it sexual then? I mean, how could he have even had…

MARGARET. I…

ADELE.…had the strength to…

MARGARET. I was asleep, Adele.

ADELE. Asleep?

MARGARET. Do you really want me to tell you?

   Pause.

ADELE. No.

MARGARET. Well…

ADELE. Yes.

   Pause.

MARGARET. *Do* you?

ADELE. Yes! (*Beat.*) You were in bed.

MARGARET. No.

ADELE. Where were you?

MARGARET. I was in here. Your father and I'd had a fight, so I decided…

ADELE. A fight over what?

MARGARET. I don't know. We'd been drinking…

ADELE. Right.

MARGARET.…we were drunk. Something idiotic, I'm sure, but I didn't want to be anywhere near him…

ADELE.…so you decided to sleep down here.

MARGARET. That's right.

ADELE. On the sofa.

MARGARET. Well, we didn't have a spare room at the time, you see…

ADELE. Okay.

MARGARET.…so, yeah.

ADELE. So, what happened?

MARGARET (*beat*). Well, I went asleep…

ADELE. Okay.

MARGARET.…or passed out, maybe. I don't know. But at some point during the night, I could hear him talking to me.

ADELE. Jonathan.

MARGARET. Yes.

ADELE. Saying what?

MARGARET. I don't know. He was asking me something.

ADELE. But you don't know what it was.

MARGARET. Well, I wasn't awake.

ADELE. Oh, right.

MARGARET.…so…

ADELE. Sorry.

MARGARET....you know?... so his voice was very faint...

ADELE. Okay.

MARGARET....or remote. Kind of like he was speaking from a long way away. (*Beat*.) But he was repeating himself...

ADELE. Right.

MARGARET....over and over. And he sounded really sad or...

ADELE. Sad?

MARGARET....or upset, or... (*Beat*.) I don't know.

ADELE. And...

MARGARET. I haven't thought about this in, *God*...

ADELE. Okay.

MARGARET....in so *long*, Adele.

ADELE. And so, what then?

MARGARET. Well, then...

ADELE. Like, what did he actually *do* to you, Mam?

MARGARET (*beat*). Well, then I felt a weight, and I woke...

ADELE. A weight.

MARGARET. Pressing down on me.

ADELE. Right.

MARGARET....and I woke, and... (*Beat*.) and he was on top of me.

ADELE. On top of you.

MARGARET. Yes... and he was inside me, Adele.

ADELE (*pause*). What do you mean?

MARGARET. He...

ADELE. No he wasn't.

MARGARET. He was.

ADELE. That's impossible.

MARGARET. No…

ADELE. Mam.

MARGARET.…It's not impossible.

ADELE. He was eleven years old!

MARGARET. He was inside me, Adele. (*Pause*.) He had taken off my underwear and…

ADELE. No.

MARGARET. What.

ADELE. I don't believe it.

MARGARET. Adele…

ADELE. I don't. I know he was bad, but…

MARGARET. Yes.

ADELE. Huh?

MARGARET. Yes. You know he was bad.

ADELE.…but he wasn't capable of… I mean, how could anyone…

MARGARET (*beat*). Adele.

ADELE.…a child. How could a boy…

MARGARET. Adele.

ADELE (*beat*). What?

MARGARET. It happened, love. (*Pause*.) It happened. And that's why your father called him the things he called him and that's the reason we've always been so vague about that night, so, I dunno…

ADELE. Evasive.

MARGARET. Yes… and that's the reason I was so upset, do you understand?

Long pause.

ADELE. I don't know what to say, Mam.

MARGARET. That's okay.

ADELE. You should have told me.

MARGARET. I know.

ADELE. Why didn't you?

MARGARET. How do you even begin to broach something like that? (*Pause*.) How? And what would the point have been except to upset you?

ADELE. I…

MARGARET. To upset us all.

Silence.

Are you okay?

ADELE. How can you not hate him?

MARGARET. How can I?

ADELE. Or not be glad he's gone.

MARGARET. Because he's my child, darling. How can I hate my child?

Silence.

ADELE. I'm sorry, Mam.

MARGARET. For what?

ADELE. I don't know. (*Beat*.) For the things I said.

MARGARET. That's okay.

ADELE. For the things I *thought*.

MARGARET. That's okay, love.

ADELE (*beat*). But I didn't really.

MARGARET. What?

ADELE. Think them. It's just…

MARGARET. I know.

ADELE.…you know? I…

MARGARET. You were a child.

ADELE. Exactly.

MARGARET. And you…

ADELE. Exactly. I *was* a child. I *was*. But you get, I don't know, an idea into your head…

MARGARET. I know.

ADELE. …you know? A notion, and…

MARGARET. Right.

ADELE. …and I was so fucking *angry* at him, Mam.

MARGARET. Who?

ADELE. Dad. Well, I was angry at everyone, actually, but I think, with Dad, it all just…

MARGARET. Right.

ADELE. …whatever…

MARGARET. …exploded.

ADELE. He said to me… Yeah, exactly. He…

MARGARET. What did he say?

ADELE. …He said I was going through a very emotional time, and…

MARGARET. This is the other day.

ADELE. Yeah.

MARGARET. Right.

ADELE. …and so I accused him of patronising me…

MARGARET. Okay.

ADELE. …but…

Pause.

MARGARET. What? (*Pause.*) What, love?

Starting to cry:

ADELE. …I *am* going through a very emotional time.

MARGARET. Oh, darling…

ADELE. I *am*.

MARGARET.…Oh, I know you are.

She reaches across the table and holds her hand.

I know.

ADELE *continues to cry. After several moments:*

You have to start talking to us, Adele.

ADELE. What?!

MARGARET. To your dad and me.

ADELE. *I* do?!

MARGARET. Actually…

ADELE. *God*, Mam!

MARGARET. Actually, no, you're right. Because all three of us are guilty of, aren't we…?

ADELE. Yes.

MARGARET.…of keeping things to ourselves. But, in general…

ADELE. Right.

MARGARET.…you can't be keeping your problems hidden from us.

ADELE. I know.

MARGARET.…do you know?

ADELE. And I'm gonna… I *do*, and I'm gonna try harder, Mam.

MARGARET. Are you?

ADELE. Yes.

MARGARET. Do you promise?

ADELE. You know what it is? Yes, I do. But, you know what happens? I get scared of putting stress on you.

MARGARET. Stress.

ADELE. Or worry.

MARGARET. Why?

ADELE. I don't know.

MARGARET (*beat*). But we'd rather *have* the worry, love…

ADELE. You'd rather…

MARGARET. Yes… than have to *wonder* all the time, you know? (*Beat.*) How you are…

ADELE. I suppose.

MARGARET.…how you're feeling…

ADELE. Does he hate me, Mam?

MARGARET. Who?

ADELE. Dad.

MARGARET. Adele…

ADELE. If you'd heard the things I…

MARGARET. All he wants is for *you* not to hate *him*.

ADELE. I don't.

MARGARET. I know. Or mistrust him.

ADELE. I'm such a fucking idiot. (*Pause.*) That's the thing, I mean, here's me accusing him of being, like, the worst of them all, and, in fact, he's the, isn't he…?

MARGARET. What.

ADELE.…the best.

MARGARET. God, I don't know about *that*, Adele.

ADELE. But, you know what I mean. All the things you've been through, the both of you, and still you're together.

MARGARET. Mm. Well, I can't say it hasn't been tough at times.

ADELE. I know it has.

MARGARET. And still is.

ADELE. But that's what I'm saying. Even in spite of all that, you've survived…

MARGARET. Uh-huh.

ADELE.…you've endured, and continue to. Where the hell are the men like Dad, you know?

MARGARET. Mm.

ADELE (*pause*).…Or the women like you. Sorry, Mam.

MARGARET. That's okay.

Silence.

Do you want some more tea?

ADELE. No, thanks.

MARGARET. Or coffee?

ADELE. No, sure I'll have to head soon, actually.

MARGARET. Really.

ADELE. Yeah, I've a couple of things to get done for work in the morning.

MARGARET. Oh. That's a shame.

Silence.

ADELE. He was good as well, though, wasn't he?

MARGARET. Who was?

ADELE. Jonathan.

MARGARET. Oh, of *course*.

ADELE. I mean, loving and…

MARGARET. *Absolutely*, Adele. Do you not remember that?

ADELE. Not really, no.

Long pause.

Or…

MARGARET. What?

ADELE....there's one time I *do* remember, actually.

MARGARET. Is there?

ADELE. Yeah. We were down in Baltimore...

MARGARET. Right.

ADELE....fishing for crabs one day. And...

MARGARET. I can't believe you haven't forgotten all that.

ADELE. Well, most of it I have...

MARGARET. Okay.

ADELE....but, no. This one time I remember pretty vividly, actually.

MARGARET. Right. So, go on...

ADELE. So, yeah...

MARGARET....We were fishing for crabs...

ADELE. That's right, and we'd already caught a load. But then... Dad, I think, caught this pathetic little thing that had only a single arm... like a...

MARGARET. Right.

ADELE....and a single leg...

MARGARET. A pincer.

ADELE. Exactly. Do you remember this?

 MARGARET. I don't think so, no.

ADELE....and Jonathan didn't want to put it into the bucket with all the others because he was terrified they'd tear it apart. So...

MARGARET. Right.

ADELE....so he threw it back into the sea. But, as it was flying through the air, a seagull swooped in and caught it...

MARGARET. *What?!*

ADELE. Do you not remember this?!

MARGARET. *No!*

ADELE. Are you sure?!

MARGARET. It *caught* it?!

ADELE. Yeah, in its beak, and just flew off. But, the image...

MARGARET. My God!

ADELE. Yeah, I know, but the image that's always there in my head, is him turned back to you... Jonathan...

MARGARET. Right.

ADELE.... turned back to you right at that moment, and his face is, it's kind of hard to describe: he looked like he was either about to get upset because he'd caused the poor crab to be eaten, or laugh because what had just happened was so kind of odd and incredible. Which of course, it was.

MARGARET. Uh-huh.

ADELE. But, yeah... (*Beat.*) So, there was this sort of expectation in his face as well, as if... I don't know, as if he was waiting to see how you'd react before he did.

Pause.

Black.

Scene Three

Several hours later. MICHAEL, dressed up from his night out, takes two small glasses and a bottle of whiskey from the press in the kitchen area and brings them to the living-room area. He sits down on the sofa, pours two glasses and takes a sip of one. MARGARET enters from upstairs in her dressing gown.

MICHAEL. Guess who was there.

MARGARET. Who?

MICHAEL. John Doyle.

MARGARET. He wasn't! Is he not sick?

MICHAEL. Yeah, I heard that as well, but he looked fairly healthy tonight, I must say.

MARGARET. Right.

She joins him on the sofa.

And did Richard enjoy it?

MICHAEL. Ah, yeah. You know Richard.

MARGARET. Mellow.

MICHAEL. Huh?

MARGARET. Mellow.

MICHAEL (*on 'Mellow'*)....Mellow. Exactly. No, it was civilised enough, now.

Long pause.

So how did it go with you?

MARGARET. Okay.

MICHAEL. Yeah?

MARGARET. Kind of.

MICHAEL. Kind of?

MARGARET. Well... (*Beat.*) she remembers, Michael.

MICHAEL. What do you mean?

MARGARET. She heard the shouting…

MICHAEL. Mine?

MARGARET. And mine.

MICHAEL (*beat*). All right.

MARGARET. She heard him pleading with you not to hurt him…

MICHAEL. And what did you tell her?

MARGARET. What do you think? I told her you never touched him.

MICHAEL. Okay.

MARGARET. I said he was giving his usual…

MICHAEL. Right.

MARGARET.…you know…

MICHAEL. Performance.

MARGARET. Yeah, and that, considering what he'd done, that it wasn't…

MICHAEL. To *you*.

MARGARET. Hm?

MICHAEL. Considering what he'd done to *you*.

MARGARET. Yes.

MICHAEL (*beat*). But you didn't tell her *what* he'd done to you.

MARGARET. I did.

MICHAEL. You didn't!

MARGARET. Sure how could I not? I had to justify what she was listening to.

MICHAEL. And what did she say?

MARGARET. She…

MICHAEL. How did she react?

MARGARET. Well, she was shocked, of course. I mean…

MICHAEL. Jesus. I can imagine.

MARGARET.…what the hell do you *do* with that kind of information, you know?

MICHAEL. Right. (*Beat.*) No, I do.

Long pause.

And so, what did she think I did, then?

MARGARET. *I* don't know.

MICHAEL. Did she think I hurt him?

MARGARET. She didn't know *what* she thought. (*Beat.*) Yes.

MICHAEL. She did.

MARGARET. You hurt him, or we were more responsible for what happened than we'd said. It was only a thought, though…

MICHAEL. Right.

MARGARET.…or, you know…

MICHAEL. A suspicion.

MARGARET. No, sure not *even* that. Just a stupid… *idea* she's had in her head all these years. Anyway. I think we put it to rest.

MICHAEL. You think.

MARGARET. Well, yeah, well, how can you know for sure…

MICHAEL. So…

MARGARET.…you know?

MICHAEL. So, she wasn't satisfied.

MARGARET. No, she *was*. She *was*. And she said to tell you she's sorry as well, by the way. So, that's…

MICHAEL. Oh, really!

MARGARET. Yeah.

MICHAEL. Well, *that's* good.

MARGARET. No, it *is*. But, *I* don't know…

MICHAEL. Okay.

MARGARET. …We'll see. She's dealing with so much stuff at the moment, so…

MICHAEL. True.

MARGARET. …you know? Belinda…

MICHAEL. Right.

MARGARET. …Dennis…

MICHAEL. Any word from Dennis?

MARGARET. She saw him.

MICHAEL. She didn't!

MARGARET. She did, yeah. Went to the pub where he works and forced him to speak to her.

MICHAEL. Wow. And what did he say?

MARGARET. He told her he just wasn't ready to commit.

MICHAEL. Okay.

MARGARET. That's it, really.

MICHAEL. Didn't mention you.

MARGARET. No, no.

MICHAEL. Or what happened here.

MARGARET. God, no, nothing like that.

MICHAEL. And have *you* heard anything from him?

MARGARET. No.

MICHAEL. You will.

MARGARET. We'll see.

MICHAEL. You *know* you will.

MARGARET. And if I do, I'll deal with him without any help from you, isn't that right?

MICHAEL. Mm.

MARGARET. Michael…

MICHAEL. Yes!

Long pause.

So, what should I do, should I give her a shout tomorrow?
Or…

MARGARET. Oh, *do*, yeah.

MICHAEL. Right.

MARGARET. But be prepared to talk about, you know…

MICHAEL.…whatever.

MARGARET. Yeah.

MICHAEL. Fair enough.

MARGARET.…to answer any questions she might want to ask
you.

MICHAEL (*pause*). Did she ask *you* many?

MARGARET. Yeah, a few.

MICHAEL. Like what?

MARGARET. Like, how I could sleep where it happened?

MICHAEL. On the sofa, you mean.

MARGARET. Mm-hm.

MICHAEL. And what did you tell her?

MARGARET. I told her it never really occurred to me to be
bothered by it.

MICHAEL (*pause*). That's funny.

MARGARET. Mm.

MICHAEL. Or is it?

MARGARET (*pause*). I don't know. (*Pause.*) She asked me…
We were discussing Belinda, you know? And she wanted to
know if I'd ever thought about suicide…

MICHAEL. Right.

MARGARET.…and…

MICHAEL. Really?

MARGARET. Yeah, and… Well, you know, that kind of being the topic of conversation.

MICHAEL. Of course.

MARGARET (*pause*). But she was genuinely worried, the poor thing.

MICHAEL. And what did you tell her?

MARGARET. You know what I told her. No.

MICHAEL. Right.

MARGARET. Never, I told her. I said it just wasn't in my nature.

MICHAEL. And is it still not?

MARGARET (*beat*). Why, are you worried?

MICHAEL. Well, we haven't had this kind of a chat in a while.

MARGARET. That's true.

MICHAEL. And things can change.

MARGARET. Or how we feel about things.

MICHAEL. That's right.

MARGARET. That's true. Well, how *I* feel hasn't changed.

MICHAEL. All right. About what?

MARGARET. About whatever. Suicide…

MICHAEL. Right.

MARGARET.…you…

MICHAEL. What do you mean?

MARGARET. How I feel about *you* hasn't changed.

Long pause.

MICHAEL. I'm so sorry, Margaret.

MARGARET. Sorry for what? (*Long pause.*) Michael…

MICHAEL. I…

MARGARET.…Listen: I'm gonna go upstairs if you start that kind of talk, all right?

MICHAEL. Why?

MARGARET. Because I don't want to hear it.

MICHAEL. Yeah, but…

MARGARET.…Or get into it.

MICHAEL. Why, though?

MARGARET. Why?

MICHAEL. Yeah.

MARGARET. Why do you *want* to?

MICHAEL. I don't know…

MARGARET. Every time you get drunk.

MICHAEL. I'm a *tiny* bit drunk.

MARGARET. Or maudlin.

MICHAEL. Well, because you're not the only one in this.

MARGARET (*pause*). Who said I was?

MICHAEL. Nobody.

MARGARET. Michael.

MICHAEL. What?

MARGARET. I *know* I'm not the only one in this.

MICHAEL. Right. So let me say what I need to say, then.

MARGARET. All right, then. Say what you need to say.

   Long pause.

MICHAEL. I'm sorry.

MARGARET. Okay.

MICHAEL. It's my fucking fault we're here…

MARGARET. Michael…

MICHAEL. Stop.

MARGARET. Okay.

MICHAEL.…that we're here and that things are the way they are. You say that how you feel about me hasn't changed, but every fucking day, I look at you and ask myself, even now, even after all this time, 'How can she not hate me for what I did? For what I made of her life. How can she do anything but despise me, and *does* she despise me?' Because, if you *do*…

MARGARET. Do I?

MICHAEL. And have you all these years? Because, if you *have*…

MARGARET. Michael. Why the hell are you saying this?

MICHAEL. I'm saying it…

MARGARET. Why?

MICHAEL.…because… Well, I'm telling you.

MARGARET. Right.

MICHAEL.…I'm saying it because there are days I look at you and I wanna…

MARGARET (*pause*). What?

MICHAEL. I dunno.

MARGARET. Michael. (*Pause.*) You want to what?

MICHAEL. You're not the one who killed him, Margaret.

MARGARET. So?

MICHAEL. I am.

MARGARET. And so what do you want to do when you look at me? (*Pause.*) Leave me?

MICHAEL. No!

MARGARET. Are you sure? Because, if you do, then you should.

MICHAEL. Margaret…

MARGARET. Seriously.

MICHAEL.…Come on.

MARGARET. Well, you're the one who wanted to talk, Michael. (*Beat*.) And I said it to you before…

MICHAEL. I know, and…

MARGARET.…didn't I?

MICHAEL. Yes. Many times.

MARGARET.…and I meant it. (*Beat*.) And I mean it now. If you wanted to go, I'd never… Michael…

MICHAEL. What?

MARGARET.…I would never hate you for it. Or resent you or judge you in any way. Ever. Do you understand? (*Beat*.) Do you hear me?

MICHAEL. I…

MARGARET. Do you?

MICHAEL. Yes, but why are you talking that way? I don't fucking want to go and *you* don't want me to go.

MARGARET. Do I not?

MICHAEL (*beat*). What do you mean?

MARGARET. Nothing.

MICHAEL. Margaret…

MARGARET. What?

MICHAEL.…don't say 'nothing' as if you're not gonna tell me anyway.

MARGARET (*beat*). Well, maybe I do.

MICHAEL. Want me to go.

MARGARET. Yeah.

MICHAEL. Why?

MARGARET. Because…

MICHAEL.…hm?

MARGARET. Because you're not happy. (*Beat.*) I know you're not happy.

MICHAEL. Are you?

MARGARET. Am *I*?

MICHAEL. Yeah.

MARGARET. No, but that's not the point. I don't have a choice.

MICHAEL. Neither do I.

MARGARET. But, you see? I'm giving it to you.

Getting up.

MICHAEL. Give me a break.

MARGARET. I am.

MICHAEL. And I choose to stay.

MARGARET. But you don't.

MICHAEL. I do.

MARGARET. Michael…

MICHAEL. *You* fucking choose to stay.

MARGARET. What?

MICHAEL. *You're* the one with the choice. Not me.

MARGARET (*beat*). How am I the one with the choice?

MICHAEL. Just spend one night out of this house. One…

MARGARET. Oh, don't…

MICHAEL.…One fucking night.

MARGARET. No.

MICHAEL. Why not?

MARGARET. You know why not.

MICHAEL. Tell me again.

MARGARET. No.

MICHAEL. Tell me. (*Pause.*) Margaret...

MARGARET. Because if I do, he might never come again.

MICHAEL. And you'd rather...

MARGARET. Yes.

MICHAEL. ...endure what he does to you...

MARGARET. Why are you making me say this?

MICHAEL. Why are you telling me to go?

Pause.

You'd rather endure what he does to you...

MARGARET. Michael...

MICHAEL. ...night after night...

MARGARET. I *hate* what he does to me, Michael.

MICHAEL. I know.

MARGARET. I fucking hate it. But, yes, I'd suffer a thousand
times worse, you know I would, a *thousand* times worse,
rather than risk never seeing him again. (*Pause.*) A *thousand*
times worse, so, yes it *is* a choice that I have. It is, and it's a
choice that I've made, and I know it hurts you, but you have a
choice as well. Because I've seen something lately, Michael.

MICHAEL. You've...

MARGARET. Yes. In your eyes. For a while now. Or in your
face.

MICHAEL. Seen what?!

MARGARET. A resentment. A bitterness.

MICHAEL. Listen...

MARGARET. Directed at me. And I know it's because you
don't understand this.

MICHAEL. What?

MARGARET. That you've never understood it. And…

MICHAEL. Margaret…

MARGARET. No, and that's fine, and why the hell should you anyway? But, this being what I want, Michael, what I actually want, then why should you feel an obligation…

MICHAEL. I don't.

MARGARET.…to stay?

MICHAEL. I don't.

MARGARET. So, why *do* you, then?!

MICHAEL. Becau… (*Beat.*) All right, look… Jesus…

MARGARET.…You know?

MICHAEL. I do, but first of all, whatever it is you're seeing, you're full of shit. (*Beat.*)… all right? You're wrong…

MARGARET. But, am I?

MICHAEL. Margaret…

MARGARET. Am I? I see it in you.

MICHAEL. No you don't! (*Beat.*) You don't. You imagine it, cos it isn't fucking there! Now, look: I stay for many reasons, all right? The fact that I'm your husband for one…

MARGARET. But that means nothing. Especially…

MICHAEL. Of course it does.

MARGARET. It doesn't, Michael. Especially given our situation. Any rea… you know, reasonable description of our marriage *as* a marriage stopped being accurate years ago.

MICHAEL. Not for me.

MARGARET. Ah, Michael.

MICHAEL. Seriously. Or at least, not in how I *feel* about you.

MARGARET. How do you feel about me?

MICHAEL. I fucking love you, of course. (*Beat.*) I love you. More than I ever did, so *how* could I leave you? Why would I want to leave you?

MARGARET. I don't know.

MICHAEL. What sense would it make? I can't live without you.

MARGARET. Okay.

MICHAEL. I can't. I couldn't. (*Beat.*) Do you believe me?

MARGARET. Yes.

MICHAEL. Huh?

MARGARET. Yes!

MICHAEL. And I do understand.

MARGARET. Do you?

MICHAEL. Of course I do. (*Pause.*) Of course. (*Pause.*) And I have to say that, whatever else comes with this package, all the fucking, I don't know…

MARGARET.…the shit.

MICHAEL.…all the fucking heartache…

MARGARET. Right.

MICHAEL.…and misery, and, yes, and shit we've been living with and dealing with this last twenty fucking years… It's not enough to make me doubt for a minute, Margaret, not for a second, that I got a rare, a privileged fucking deal. (*Beat.*) I know I did, so, no. (*Beat.*) No. I'd rather not go anywhere if you don't mind.

MARGARET (*pause*). Okay.

MICHAEL.…All right?

MARGARET. Thank you.

MICHAEL. You're welcome.

MARGARET (*long pause*). Come over here.

MICHAEL. Why?

MARGARET. Just come over.

He moves to the sofa and sits down, putting his arm around her. She rests her head on his shoulder. Some time passes before:

MICHAEL. Don't fall asleep on me.

MARGARET. I'm not. What time is it?

MICHAEL. Twenty to.

MARGARET. All right.

Long pause.

All right. I'm going to get ready.

MICHAEL. Okay.

She gets up and goes out to the stairs, exits up them. After a moment, MICHAEL gets up and exits to the utility area. He returns with bedclothes with which he makes up the sofa bed. As he is finishing, MARGARET re-enters from upstairs. She takes off her dressing gown. MICHAEL pulls the duvet back and she gets in. He sits on the edge of the bed, then leans down and kisses her forehead.

Goodnight.

MARGARET. I love you too.

MICHAEL. Hm?

MARGARET. I love you too. (*Beat.*) *Also* more than I ever did.

She reaches up and touches his cheek with her hand.

And we'll always have our days…

MICHAEL. Right.

MARGARET.…won't we?

MICHAEL. Absolutely.

Long pause.

I'll see you tomorrow.

MARGARET. See you tomorrow.

He gets up, goes to the door to the hallway, switches off the main light, then exits, switching off the lamp in the hall before heading up the stairs. MARGARET just lies there, illuminated now only by the lamp beside the sofa bed.

Silence. Finally, she reaches out and switches it off, leaving the stage in darkness. Another silence. A child's voice whispers plaintively:

VOICE. Mammy…

Pause.

Mammy…

Fade up, with a familiar vague and abstract light, to reveal a young boy, dressed only in his underwear, standing over the bed.

Why don't you love me, Mammy?

MARGARET, *eyes closed, unmoving, doesn't respond.*

Why don't you love me?

Pause.

Mammy…!

Black.

A Nick Hern Book

Our Few and Evil Days first published in Great Britain in 2014 as a paperback original by Nick Hern Books Limited, The Glasshouse, 49a Goldhawk Road, London W12 8QP in association with the Abbey Theatre, Dublin

Our Few and Evil Days copyright © 2014 Mark O'Rowe

Mark O'Rowe has asserted his moral right to be identified as the author of this work

Cover photograph of Sinéad Cusack, Ciarán Hinds and Charlie Murphy by Sarah Doyle

Designed and typeset by Nick Hern Books, London
Printed in Great Britain by CPI Group (UK) Ltd

A CIP catalogue record for this book is available from the British Library

ISBN 978 1 84842 446 3

www.nickhernbooks.co.uk

facebook.com/nickhernbooks

twitter.com/nickhernbooks